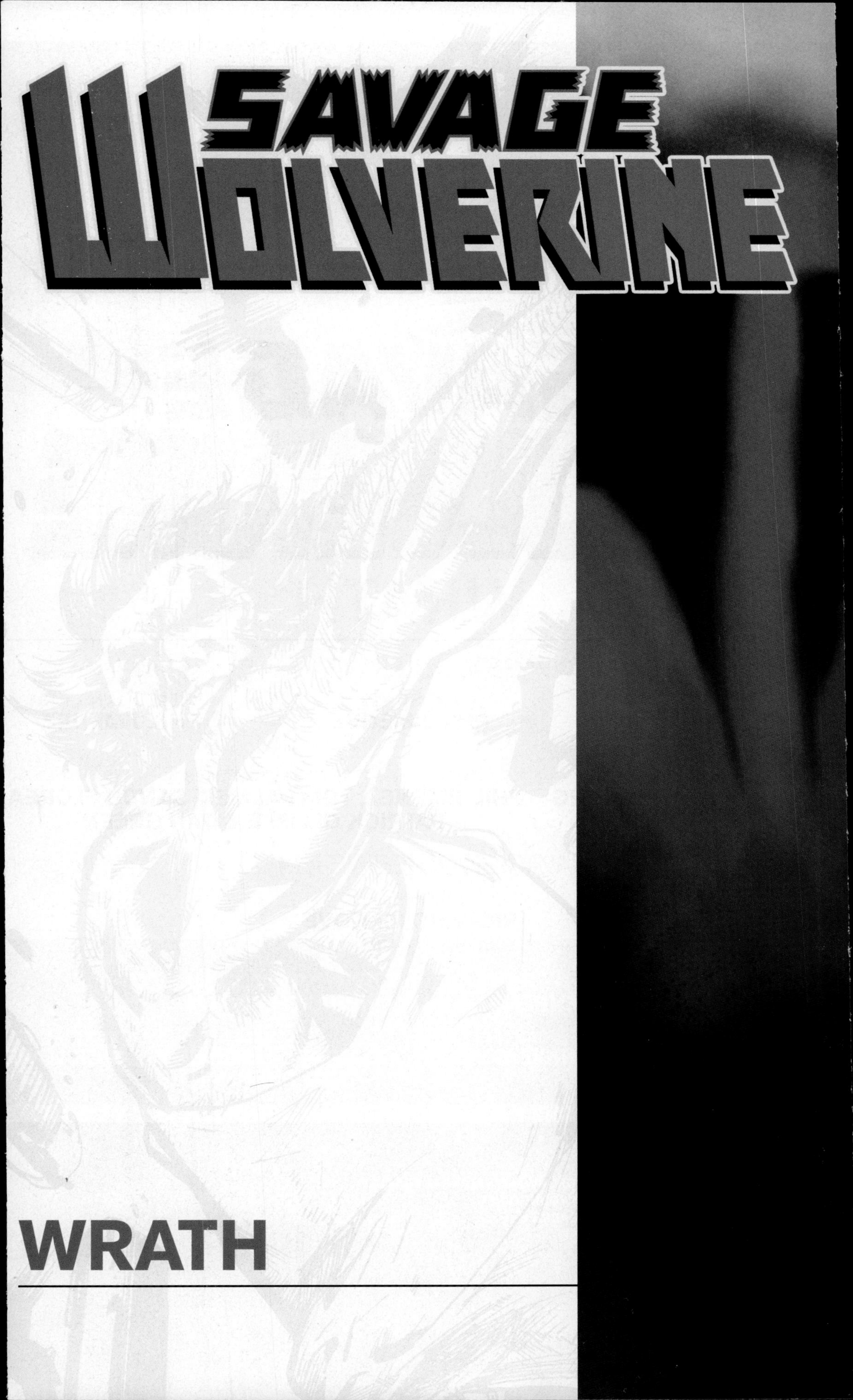

SAVAGE WOLVERINE

WRATH

SAVAGE WOLVERINE
WRATH

SAVAGE WOLVERINE #12-13

WRITERS
**PHIL JIMENEZ &
SCOTT LOPE**

ARTIST, #12
PHIL JIMENEZ

BREAKDOWNS, #13
PHIL JIMENEZ

COLORIST
RACHELLE ROSENBERG

FINISHED ART, #13
**PHIL JIMENEZ, TOM PALMER, SANDU FLOREA,
PATRICK OLLIFFE & DAN GREEN**

SAVAGE WOLVERINE #14-17

STORY & ART
RICHARD ISANOVE

COVER ARTISTS
PHIL JIMENEZ & FRANK D'ARMATA (#12), **PHIL JIMENEZ &
RACHELLE ROSENBERG** (#13) **AND RICHARD ISANOVE** (#14-17)

LETTERER
VC'S CORY PETIT

ASSISTANT EDITOR
FRANKIE JOHNSON

EDITORS
**JEANINE SCHAEFER &
TOM BRENNAN**

GROUP EDITOR
NICK LOWE

COLLECTION EDITOR **ALEX STARBUCK**
ASSISTANT EDITOR **SARAH BRUNSTAD**

Many years ago, a secret government organization abducted the man called Logan, a mutant possessing razor-sharp bone claws and the ability to heal from any wound. In their attempt to create the perfect living weapon, the organization bonded the unbreakable metal Adamantium to his skeleton. The process was excruciating, and by the end there was little left of the man known as Logan. He had become…

SAVAGE WOLVERINE

SAVAGE WOLVERINE VOL. 3: WRATH. Contains material originally published in magazine form as SAVAGE WOLVERINE #-17. First printing 2014. ISBN# 978-0-7851-5486-0. Published by MARVEL WORLDWIDE, INC., a subsidiary of MARVEL ENTERTAINMENT, LLC. OFFICE OF PUBLICATION: 135 West 50th Street, New York, NY 10020. Copyright © 2013 2014 Marvel Characters, Inc. All rights reserved. All characters featured in this issue and the distinctive names and likenesses thereof, and all related indicia are trademarks of Marvel Characters, Inc. No similarity between any of the names, characters, persons, and/or institutions in this magazine with those of any living or dead person or institution is intended, and any such similarity which may exist is purely coincidental. **Printed in the U.S.A.** ALAN FINE, EVP - Office the President, Marvel Worldwide, Inc. and EVP & CMO Marvel Characters B.V.; DAN BUCKLEY, Publisher & President Print, Animation & Digital Divisions; JOE QUESADA, Chief Creative Officer; TOM BREVOORT, SVP of Publishing; DAVID GABRIEL, SVP of Operations & Procurement, Publishing; C.B. CEBULSKI, SVP of Creator & Content Development; DAVID BOGART, SVP Print, Sales & Marketing; JIM O'KEEFE, VP of Operations & Logistics; DAN CARR, Executive Director of Publishing Technology; SUSAN CRESPI, Editorial Operations Manager; ALEX MORALES, Publishing Operations Manager; STAN LEE, Chairman Emeritus. For information regarding advertising in Marvel Comics or on Marvel.com, please contact Niza Disla, Director of Marvel Partnerships, at ndisla@marvel.com. For Marvel subscription inquiries, please 800-217-9158. Manufactured between 4/18/2014 and 6/2/2014 by R.R. DONNELLEY, INC., SALEM, VA, USA.

10 9 8 7 6 5 4 3 2 1

12 COME CONQUER THE BEASTS PART 1: CLAWS & TEETH

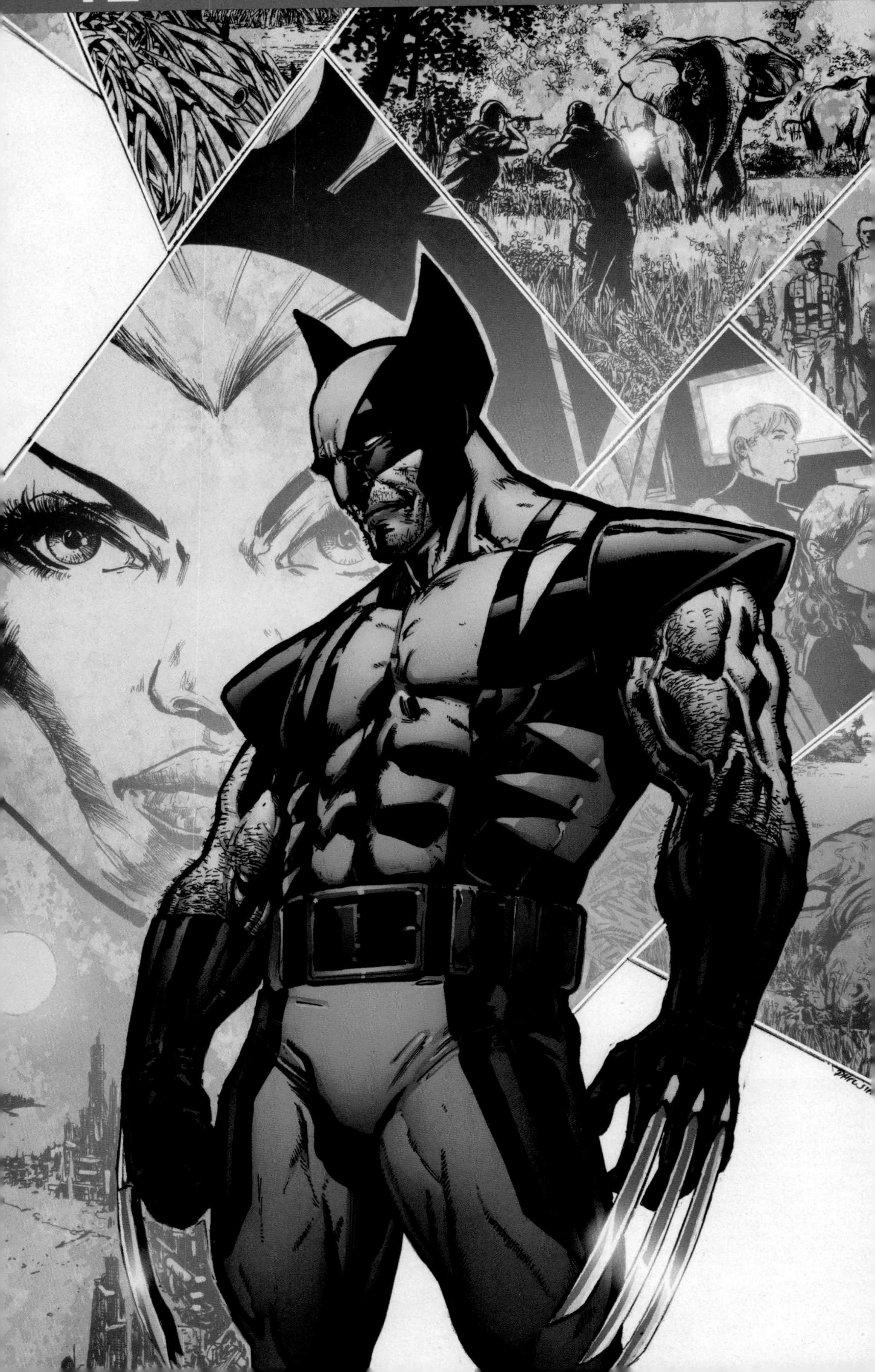

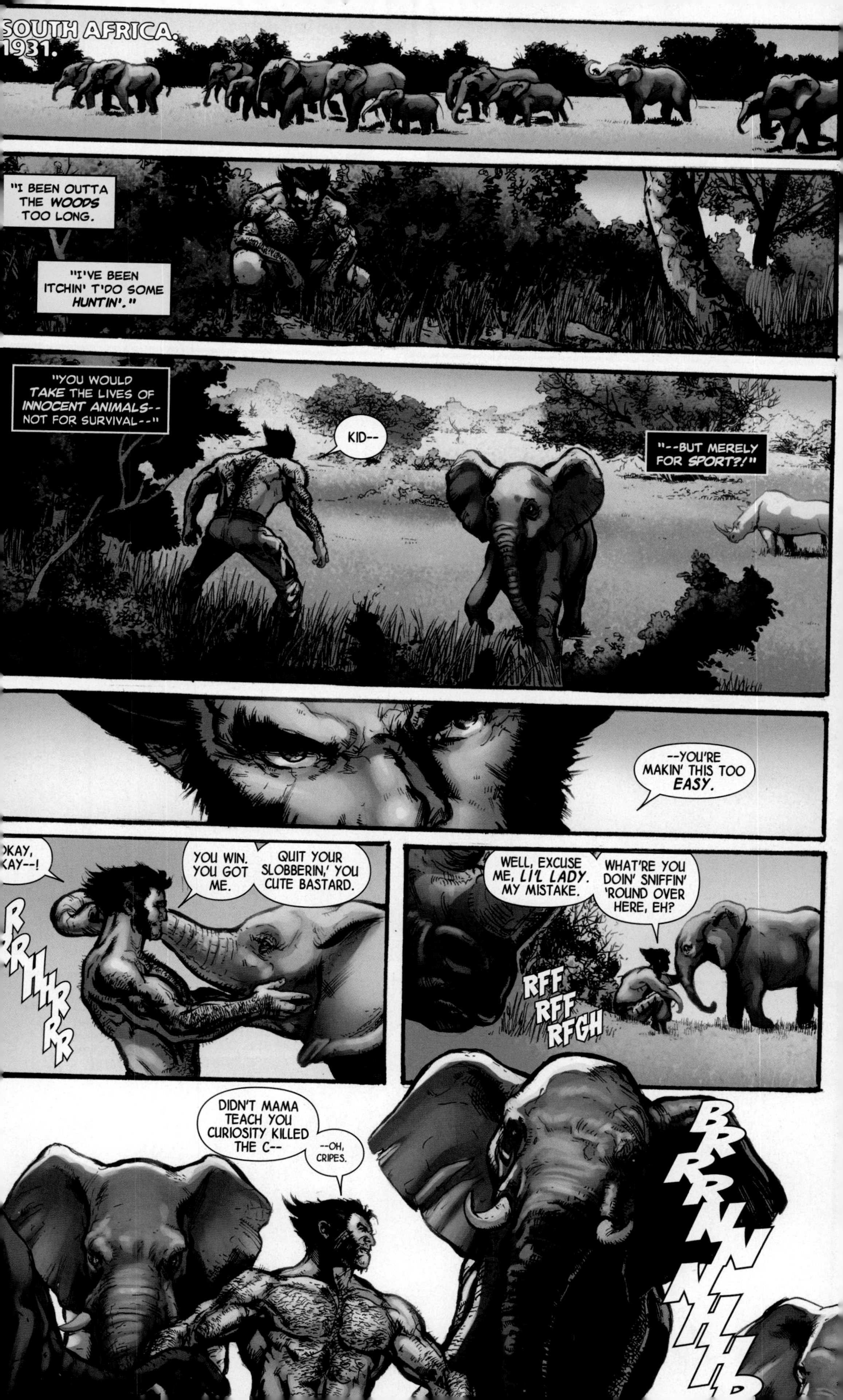

SOUTH AFRICA. 1931.
"I BEEN OUTTA THE WOODS TOO LONG.
"I'VE BEEN ITCHIN' T'DO SOME HUNTIN'."
"YOU WOULD TAKE THE LIVES OF INNOCENT ANIMALS--NOT FOR SURVIVAL--"
KID--
"--BUT MERELY FOR SPORT?!"
--YOU'RE MAKIN' THIS TOO EASY.
KAY--!
YOU WIN. YOU GOT ME.
QUIT YOUR SLOBBERIN,' YOU CUTE BASTARD.
WELL, EXCUSE ME, LI'L LADY. MY MISTAKE.
WHAT'RE YOU DOIN' SNIFFIN' 'ROUND OVER HERE, EH?
RFF RFF RFGH
DIDN'T MAMA TEACH YOU CURIOSITY KILLED THE C--
--OH, CRIPES.

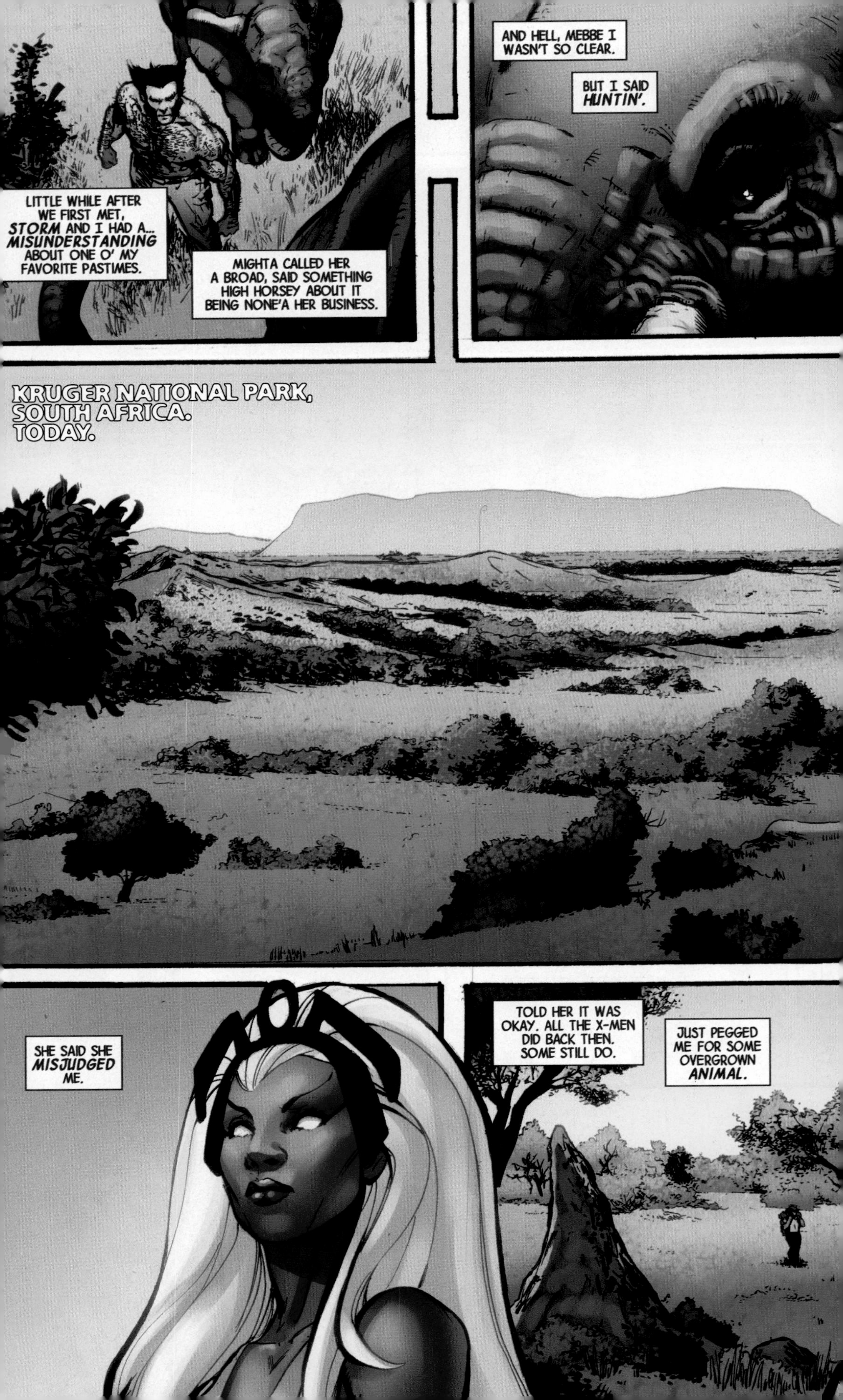
LITTLE WHILE AFTER WE FIRST MET, STORM AND I HAD A... MISUNDERSTANDING ABOUT ONE O' MY FAVORITE PASTIMES.
MIGHTA CALLED HER A BROAD, SAID SOMETHING HIGH HORSEY ABOUT IT BEING NONE'A HER BUSINESS.
AND HELL, MEBBE I WASN'T SO CLEAR.
BUT I SAID HUNTIN'.
KRUGER NATIONAL PARK, SOUTH AFRICA. TODAY.
SHE SAID SHE MISJUDGED ME.
TOLD HER IT WAS OKAY. ALL THE X-MEN DID BACK THEN. SOME STILL DO.
JUST PEGGED ME FOR SOME OVERGROWN ANIMAL.

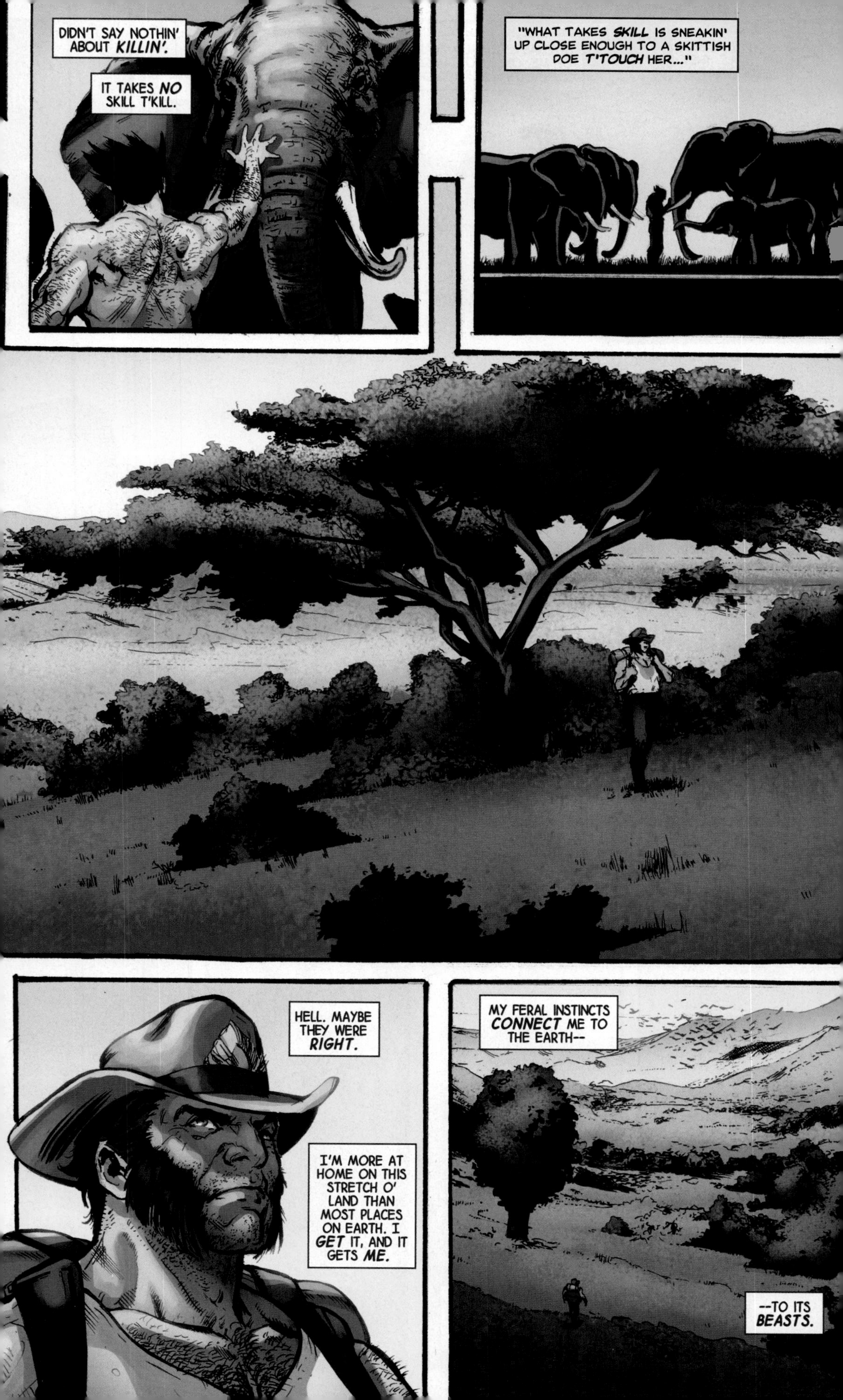
DIDN'T SAY NOTHIN' ABOUT KILLIN'.
IT TAKES NO SKILL T'KILL.
"WHAT TAKES SKILL IS SNEAKIN' UP CLOSE ENOUGH TO A SKITTISH DOE T'TOUCH HER..."
HELL. MAYBE THEY WERE RIGHT.
I'M MORE AT HOME ON THIS STRETCH O' LAND THAN MOST PLACES ON EARTH. I GET IT, AND IT GETS ME.
MY FERAL INSTINCTS CONNECT ME TO THE EARTH--
--TO ITS BEASTS.

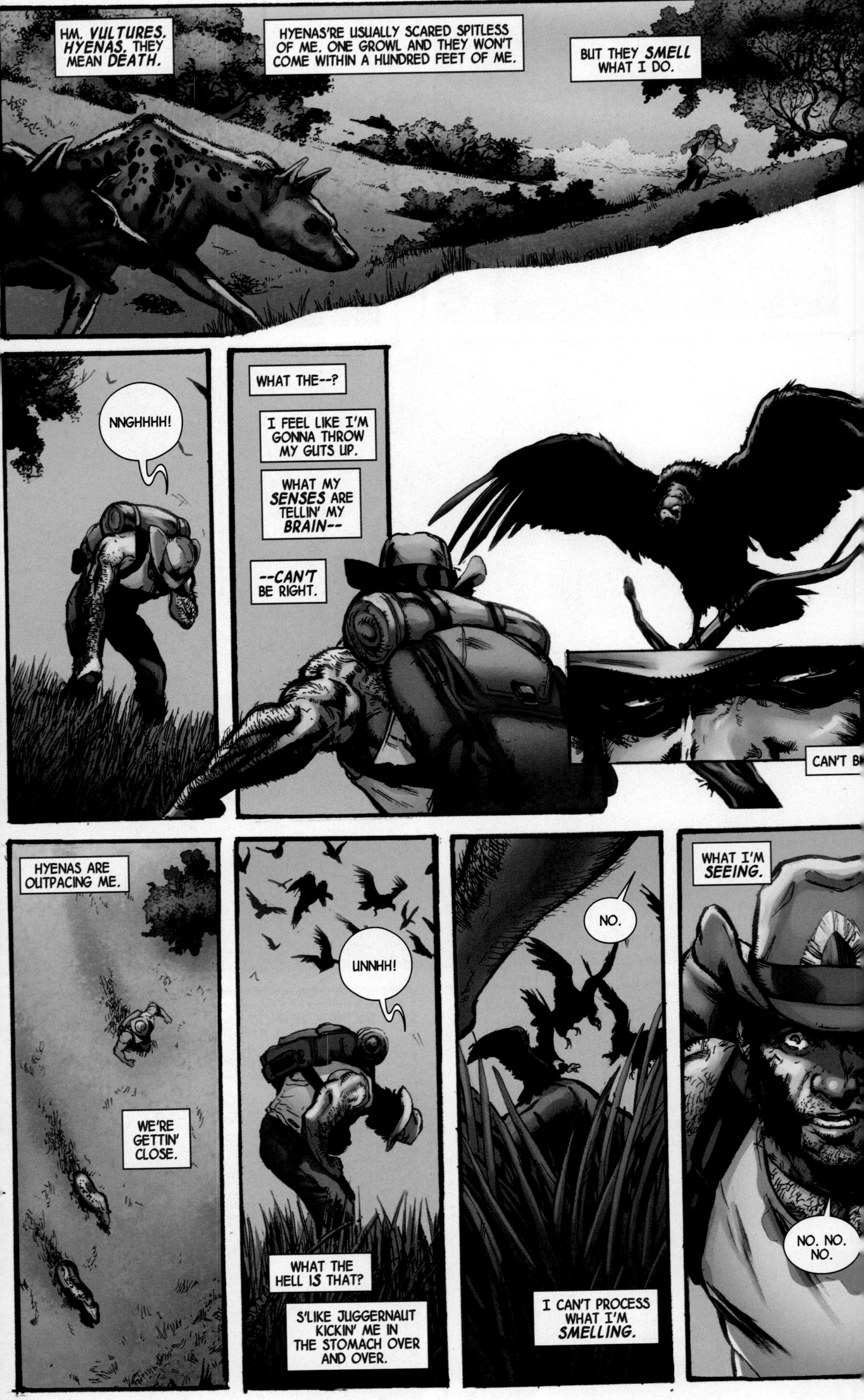
HM. VULTURES. HYENAS. THEY MEAN DEATH.
HYENAS'RE USUALLY SCARED SPITLESS OF ME. ONE GROWL AND THEY WON'T COME WITHIN A HUNDRED FEET OF ME.
BUT THEY SMELL WHAT I DO.
NNGHHHH!
WHAT THE--?
I FEEL LIKE I'M GONNA THROW MY GUTS UP.
WHAT MY SENSES ARE TELLIN' MY BRAIN--
--CAN'T BE RIGHT.
HYENAS ARE OUTPACING ME.
WE'RE GETTIN' CLOSE.
UNNHH!
WHAT THE HELL IS THAT?
S'LIKE JUGGERNAUT KICKIN' ME IN THE STOMACH OVER AND OVER.
NO.
I CAN'T PROCESS WHAT I'M SMELLING.
WHAT I'M SEEING.
NO. NO. NO.

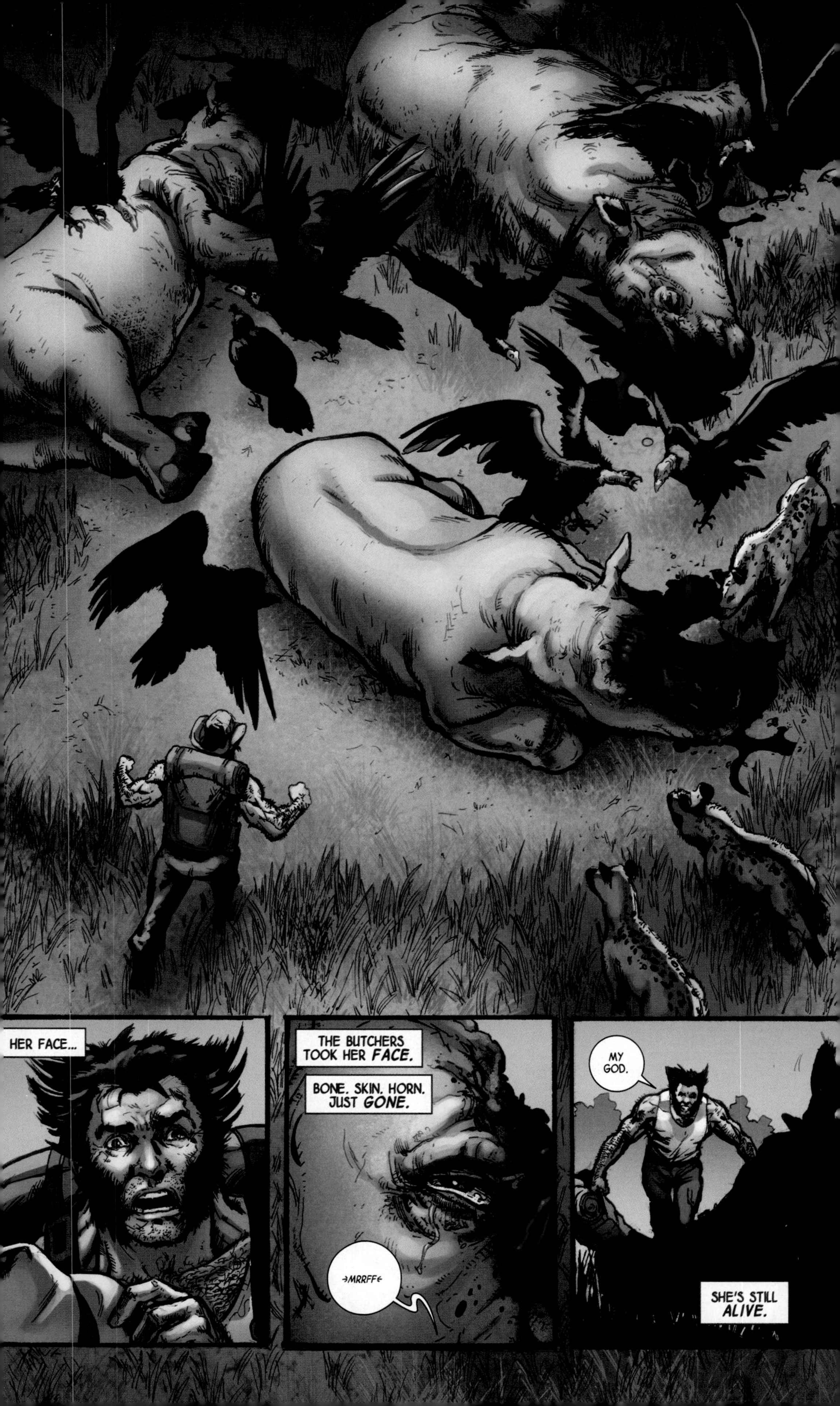
HER FACE...
THE BUTCHERS TOOK HER FACE.
BONE. SKIN. HORN. JUST GONE.
MRRFF
MY GOD.
SHE'S STILL ALIVE.

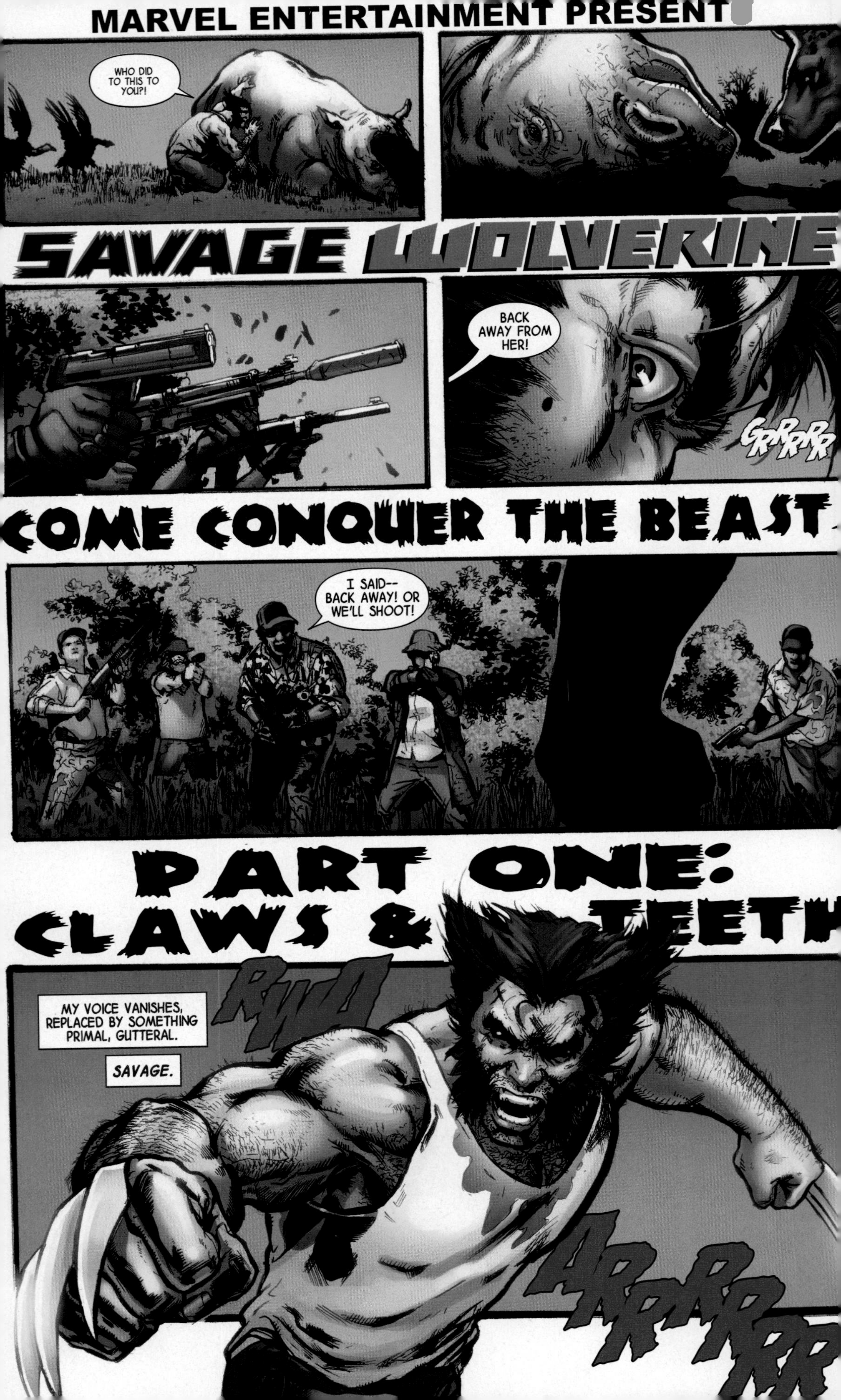
MARVEL ENTERTAINMENT PRESENT
WHO DID TO THIS TO YOU?!
SAVAGE WOLVERINE
BACK AWAY FROM HER!
GRRRRR
COME CONQUER THE BEAST
I SAID-- BACK AWAY! OR WE'LL SHOOT!
PART ONE:
CLAWS &
MY VOICE VANISHES, REPLACED BY SOMETHING PRIMAL, GUTTERAL.
SAVAGE.

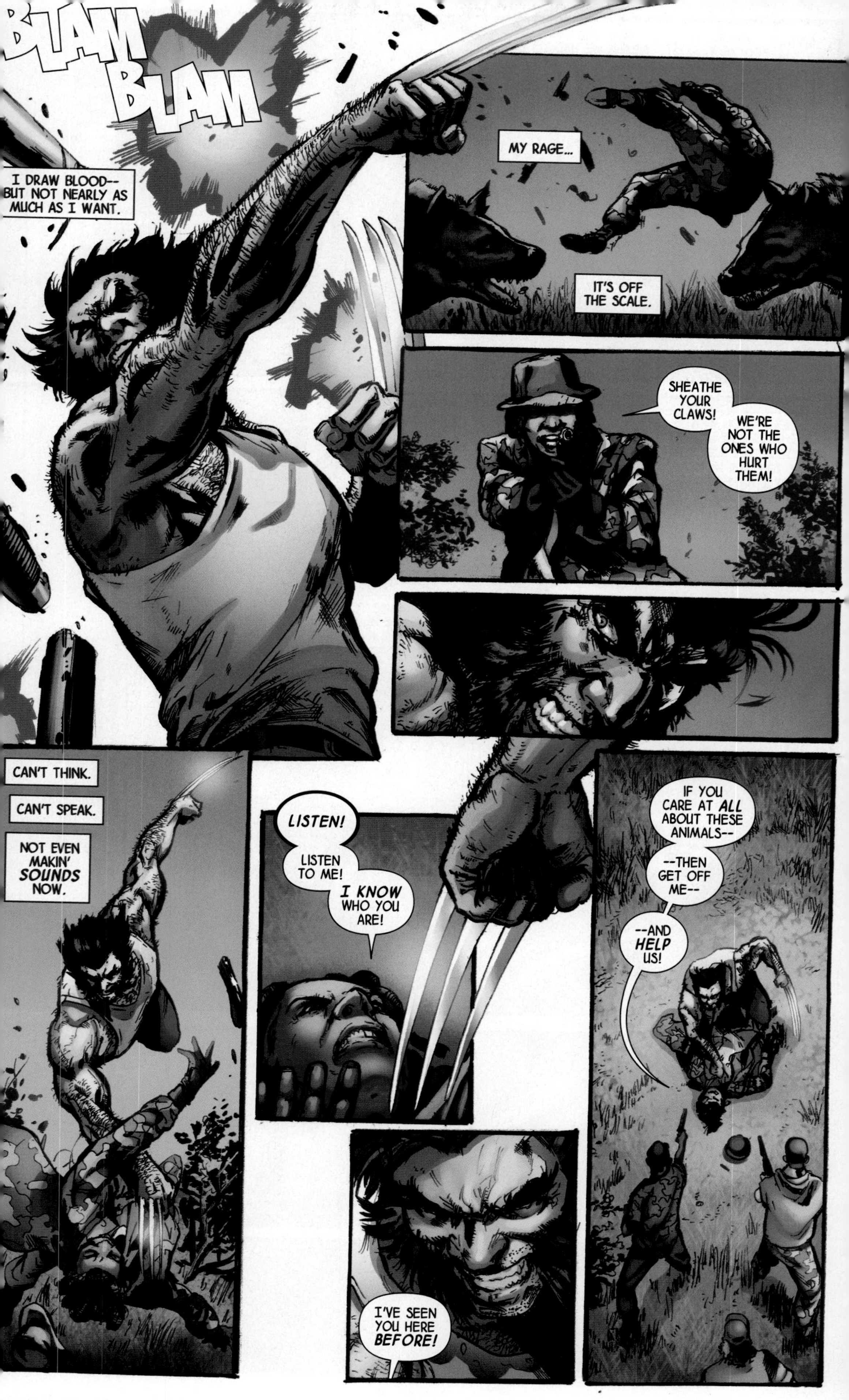
BLAM
BLAM
I DRAW BLOOD--
BUT NOT NEARLY AS
MUCH AS I WANT.
MY RAGE...
IT'S OFF
THE SCALE.
SHEATHE
YOUR
CLAWS!
WE'RE
NOT THE
ONES WHO
HURT
THEM!
CAN'T THINK.
CAN'T SPEAK.
NOT EVEN
MAKIN'
SOUNDS
NOW.
LISTEN!
LISTEN
TO ME!
I KNOW
WHO YOU
ARE!
I'VE SEEN
YOU HERE
BEFORE!
IF YOU
CARE AT ALL
ABOUT THESE
ANIMALS--
--THEN
GET OFF
ME--
--AND
HELP
US!

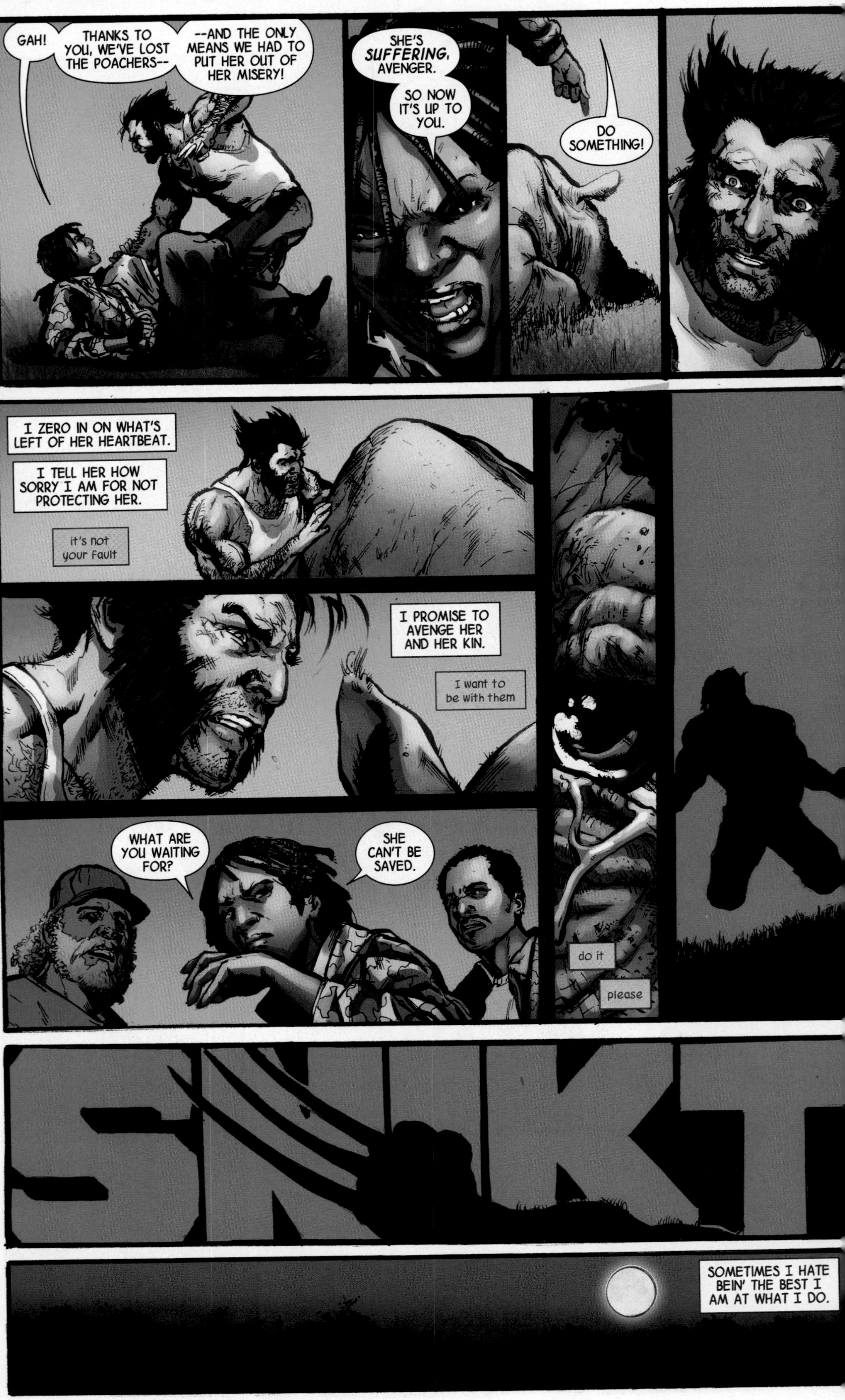
GAH!
THANKS TO YOU, WE'VE LOST THE POACHERS--
--AND THE ONLY MEANS WE HAD TO PUT HER OUT OF HER MISERY!
SHE'S SUFFERING, AVENGER.
SO NOW IT'S UP TO YOU.
DO SOMETHING!
I ZERO IN ON WHAT'S LEFT OF HER HEARTBEAT.
I TELL HER HOW SORRY I AM FOR NOT PROTECTING HER.
it's not your fault
I PROMISE TO AVENGE HER AND HER KIN.
I want to be with them
WHAT ARE YOU WAITING FOR?
SHE CAN'T BE SAVED.
do it
please
SNIKT
SOMETIMES I HATE BEIN' THE BEST I AM AT WHAT I DO.

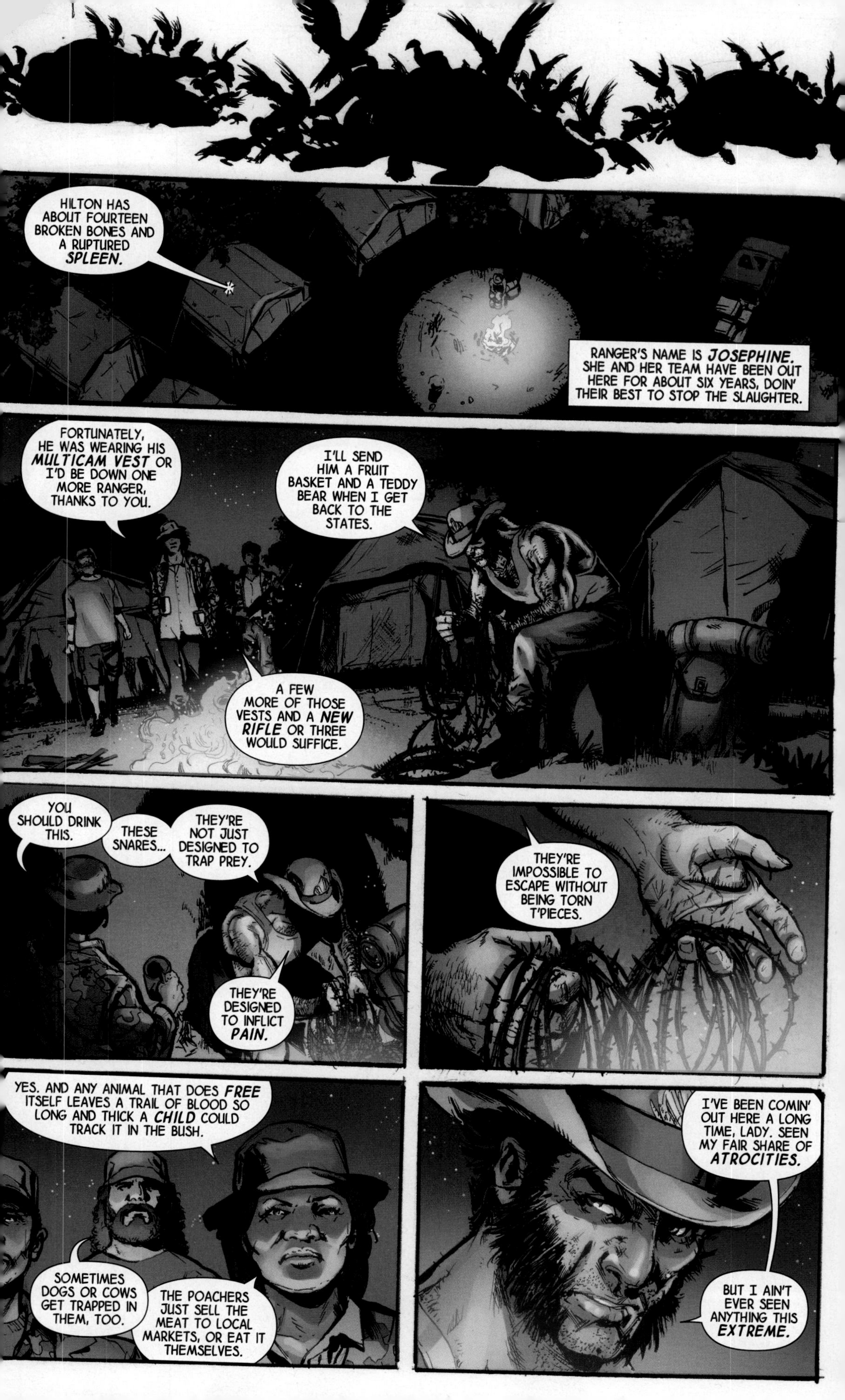
HILTON HAS ABOUT FOURTEEN BROKEN BONES AND A RUPTURED SPLEEN.
RANGER'S NAME IS JOSEPHINE. SHE AND HER TEAM HAVE BEEN OUT HERE FOR ABOUT SIX YEARS, DOIN' THEIR BEST TO STOP THE SLAUGHTER.
FORTUNATELY, HE WAS WEARING HIS MULTICAM VEST OR I'D BE DOWN ONE MORE RANGER, THANKS TO YOU.
I'LL SEND HIM A FRUIT BASKET AND A TEDDY BEAR WHEN I GET BACK TO THE STATES.
A FEW MORE OF THOSE VESTS AND A NEW RIFLE OR THREE WOULD SUFFICE.
YOU SHOULD DRINK THIS.
THESE SNARES...
THEY'RE NOT JUST DESIGNED TO TRAP PREY.
THEY'RE DESIGNED TO INFLICT PAIN.
THEY'RE IMPOSSIBLE TO ESCAPE WITHOUT BEING TORN T'PIECES.
YES. AND ANY ANIMAL THAT DOES FREE ITSELF LEAVES A TRAIL OF BLOOD SO LONG AND THICK A CHILD COULD TRACK IT IN THE BUSH.
SOMETIMES DOGS OR COWS GET TRAPPED IN THEM, TOO.
THE POACHERS JUST SELL THE MEAT TO LOCAL MARKETS, OR EAT IT THEMSELVES.
I'VE BEEN COMIN' OUT HERE A LONG TIME, LADY. SEEN MY FAIR SHARE OF ATROCITIES.
BUT I AIN'T EVER SEEN ANYTHING THIS EXTREME.

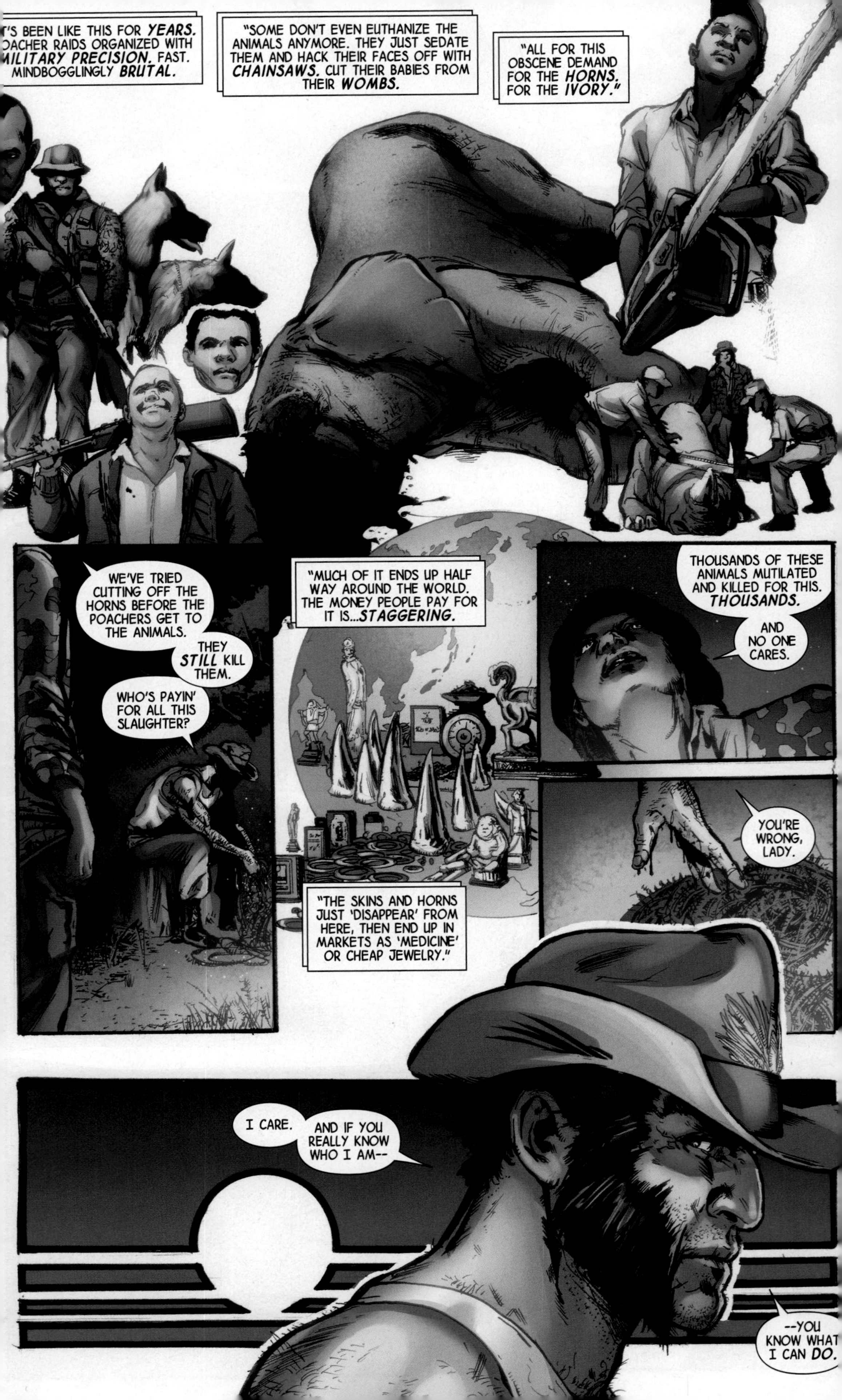
'S BEEN LIKE THIS FOR YEARS. OACHER RAIDS ORGANIZED WITH ILITARY PRECISION. FAST. MINDBOGGLINGLY BRUTAL.
"SOME DON'T EVEN EUTHANIZE THE ANIMALS ANYMORE. THEY JUST SEDATE THEM AND HACK THEIR FACES OFF WITH CHAINSAWS. CUT THEIR BABIES FROM THEIR WOMBS.
"ALL FOR THIS OBSCENE DEMAND FOR THE HORNS. FOR THE IVORY."
WE'VE TRIED CUTTING OFF THE HORNS BEFORE THE POACHERS GET TO THE ANIMALS.
THEY STILL KILL THEM.
WHO'S PAYIN' FOR ALL THIS SLAUGHTER?
"MUCH OF IT ENDS UP HALF WAY AROUND THE WORLD. THE MONEY PEOPLE PAY FOR IT IS...STAGGERING.
"THE SKINS AND HORNS JUST 'DISAPPEAR' FROM HERE, THEN END UP IN MARKETS AS 'MEDICINE' OR CHEAP JEWELRY."
THOUSANDS OF THESE ANIMALS MUTILATED AND KILLED FOR THIS. THOUSANDS.
AND NO ONE CARES.
YOU'RE WRONG, LADY.
I CARE.
AND IF YOU REALLY KNOW WHO I AM--
--YOU KNOW WHAT I CAN DO.

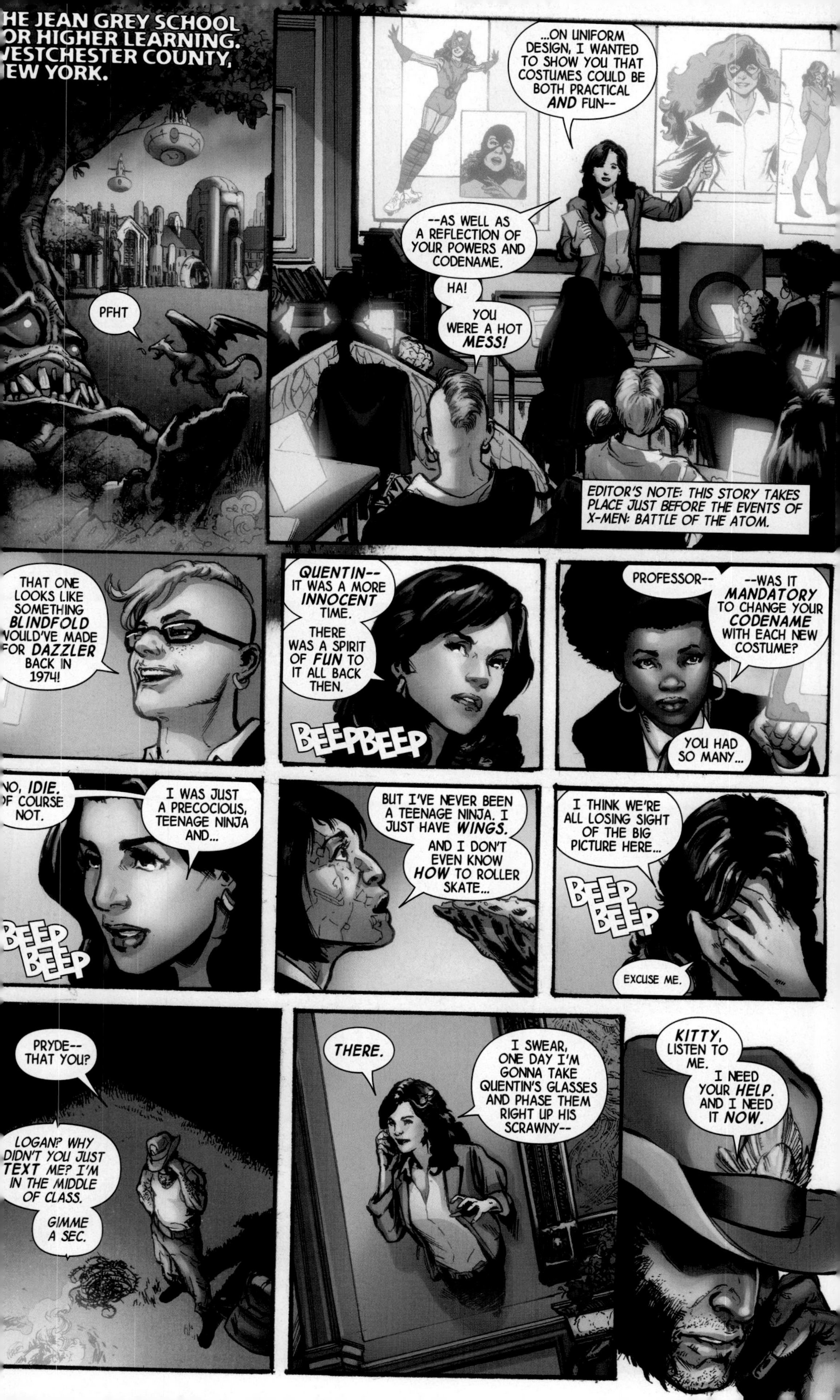

HE JEAN GREY SCHOOL
OR HIGHER LEARNING.
VESTCHESTER COUNTY,
EW YORK.
PFHT
...ON UNIFORM DESIGN, I WANTED TO SHOW YOU THAT COSTUMES COULD BE BOTH PRACTICAL AND FUN--
--AS WELL AS A REFLECTION OF YOUR POWERS AND CODENAME.
HA!
YOU WERE A HOT MESS!
EDITOR'S NOTE: THIS STORY TAKES PLACE JUST BEFORE THE EVENTS OF X-MEN: BATTLE OF THE ATOM.
THAT ONE LOOKS LIKE SOMETHING BLINDFOLD WOULD'VE MADE FOR DAZZLER BACK IN 1974!
QUENTIN-- IT WAS A MORE INNOCENT TIME.
THERE WAS A SPIRIT OF FUN TO IT ALL BACK THEN.
BEEPBEEP
PROFESSOR--
--WAS IT MANDATORY TO CHANGE YOUR CODENAME WITH EACH NEW COSTUME?
YOU HAD SO MANY...
NO, IDIE. OF COURSE NOT.
I WAS JUST A PRECOCIOUS, TEENAGE NINJA AND...
BEEP BEEP
BUT I'VE NEVER BEEN A TEENAGE NINJA. I JUST HAVE WINGS.
AND I DON'T EVEN KNOW HOW TO ROLLER SKATE...
I THINK WE'RE ALL LOSING SIGHT OF THE BIG PICTURE HERE...
BEEP BEEP
EXCUSE ME.
PRYDE-- THAT YOU?
LOGAN? WHY DIDN'T YOU JUST TEXT ME? I'M IN THE MIDDLE OF CLASS.
GIMME A SEC.
THERE.
I SWEAR, ONE DAY I'M GONNA TAKE QUENTIN'S GLASSES AND PHASE THEM RIGHT UP HIS SCRAWNY--
KITTY, LISTEN TO ME.
I NEED YOUR HELP. AND I NEED IT NOW.

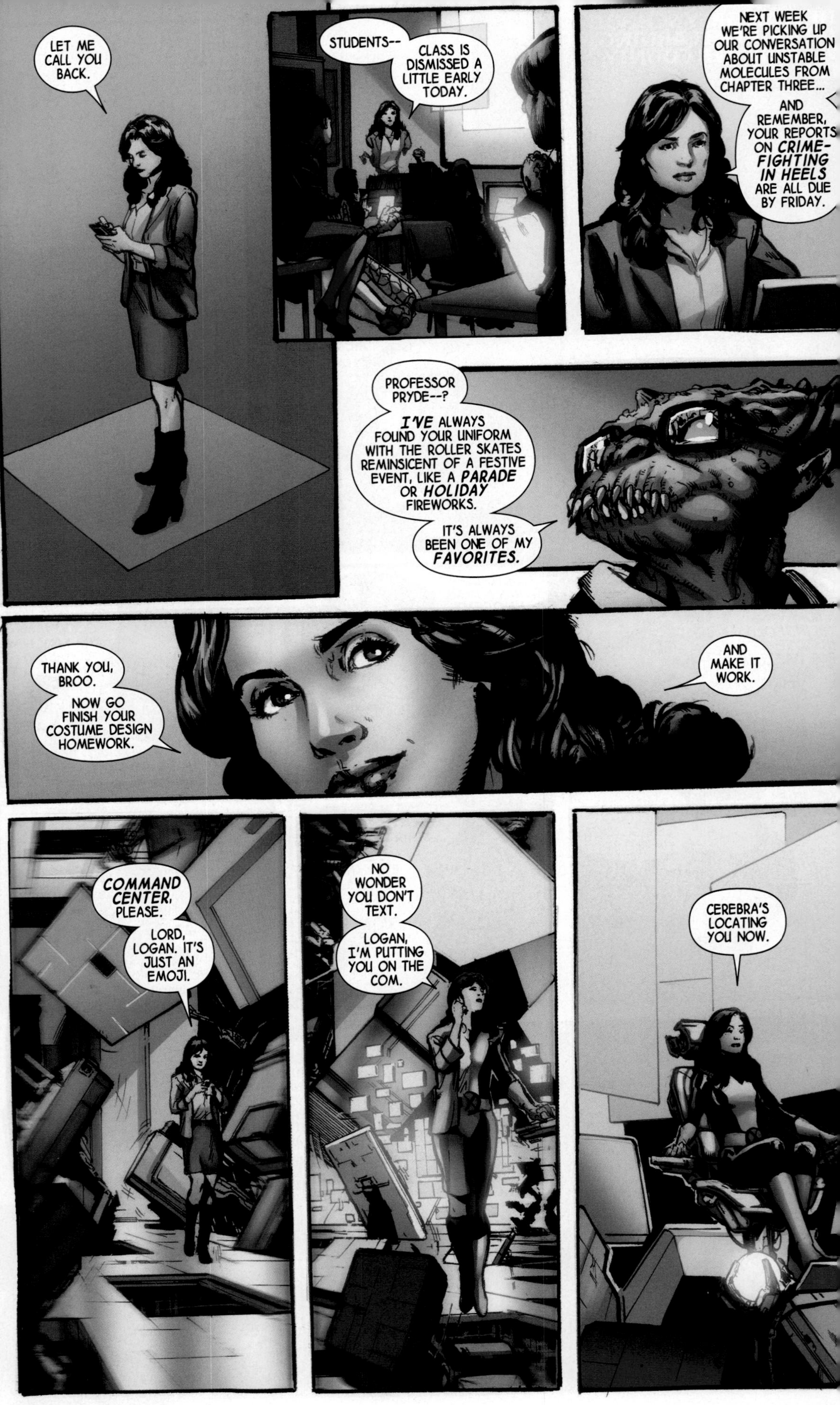
LET ME CALL YOU BACK.
STUDENTS--
CLASS IS DISMISSED A LITTLE EARLY TODAY.
NEXT WEEK WE'RE PICKING UP OUR CONVERSATION ABOUT UNSTABLE MOLECULES FROM CHAPTER THREE...
AND REMEMBER, YOUR REPORTS ON CRIME-FIGHTING IN HEELS ARE ALL DUE BY FRIDAY.
PROFESSOR PRYDE--?
I'VE ALWAYS FOUND YOUR UNIFORM WITH THE ROLLER SKATES REMINISCENT OF A FESTIVE EVENT, LIKE A PARADE OR HOLIDAY FIREWORKS.
IT'S ALWAYS BEEN ONE OF MY FAVORITES.
THANK YOU, BROO.
NOW GO FINISH YOUR COSTUME DESIGN HOMEWORK.
AND MAKE IT WORK.
COMMAND CENTER, PLEASE.
LORD, LOGAN. IT'S JUST AN EMOJI.
NO WONDER YOU DON'T TEXT.
LOGAN, I'M PUTTING YOU ON THE COM.
CEREBRA'S LOCATING YOU NOW.

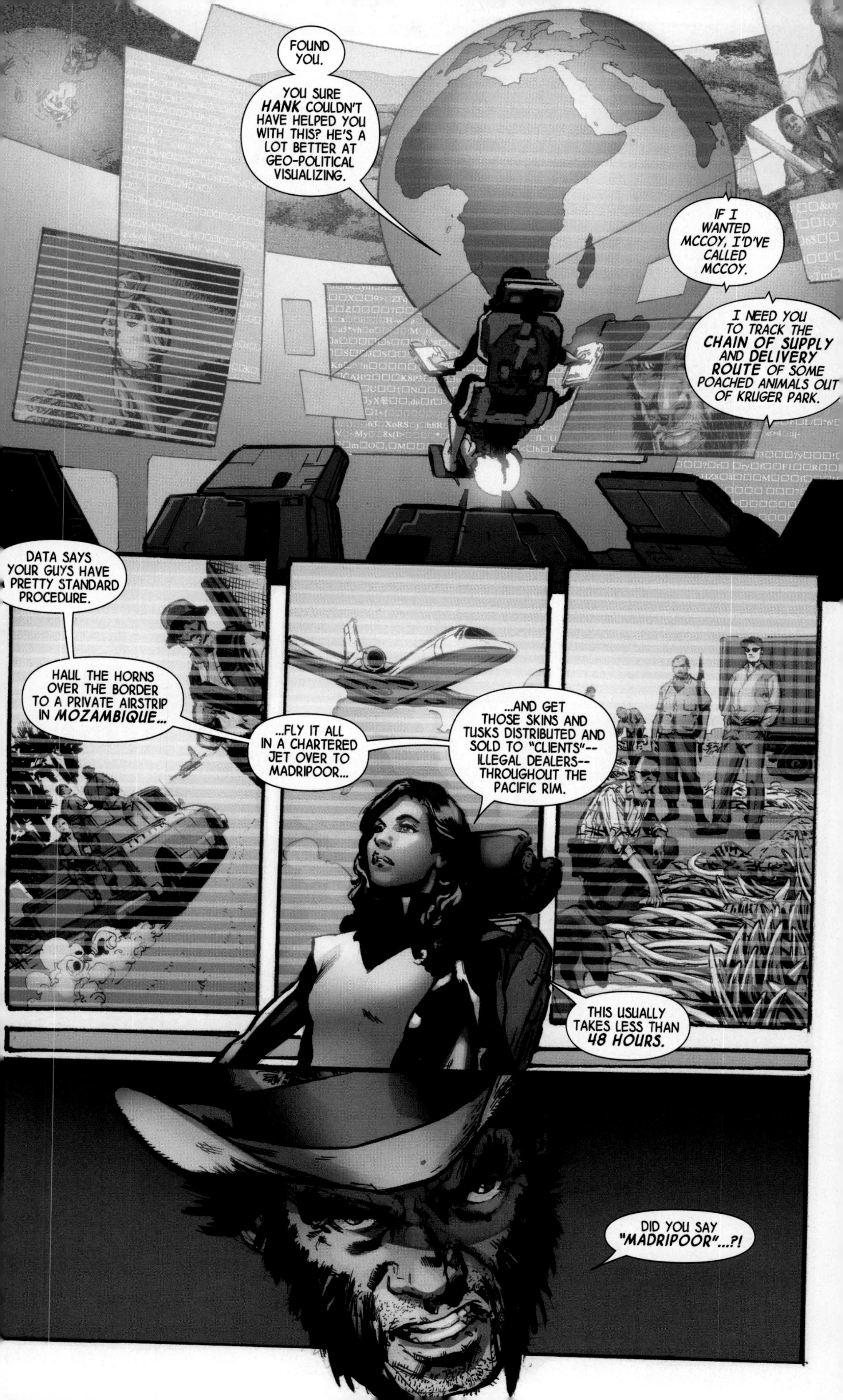
FOUND YOU.
YOU SURE HANK COULDN'T HAVE HELPED YOU WITH THIS? HE'S A LOT BETTER AT GEO-POLITICAL VISUALIZING.
IF I WANTED MCCOY, I'D'VE CALLED MCCOY.
I NEED YOU TO TRACK THE CHAIN OF SUPPLY AND DELIVERY ROUTE OF SOME POACHED ANIMALS OUT OF KRUGER PARK.
DATA SAYS YOUR GUYS HAVE PRETTY STANDARD PROCEDURE.
HAUL THE HORNS OVER THE BORDER TO A PRIVATE AIRSTRIP IN MOZAMBIQUE...
...FLY IT ALL IN A CHARTERED JET OVER TO MADRIPOOR...
...AND GET THOSE SKINS AND TUSKS DISTRIBUTED AND SOLD TO "CLIENTS"-- ILLEGAL DEALERS-- THROUGHOUT THE PACIFIC RIM.
THIS USUALLY TAKES LESS THAN 48 HOURS.
DID YOU SAY "MADRIPOOR"...?!

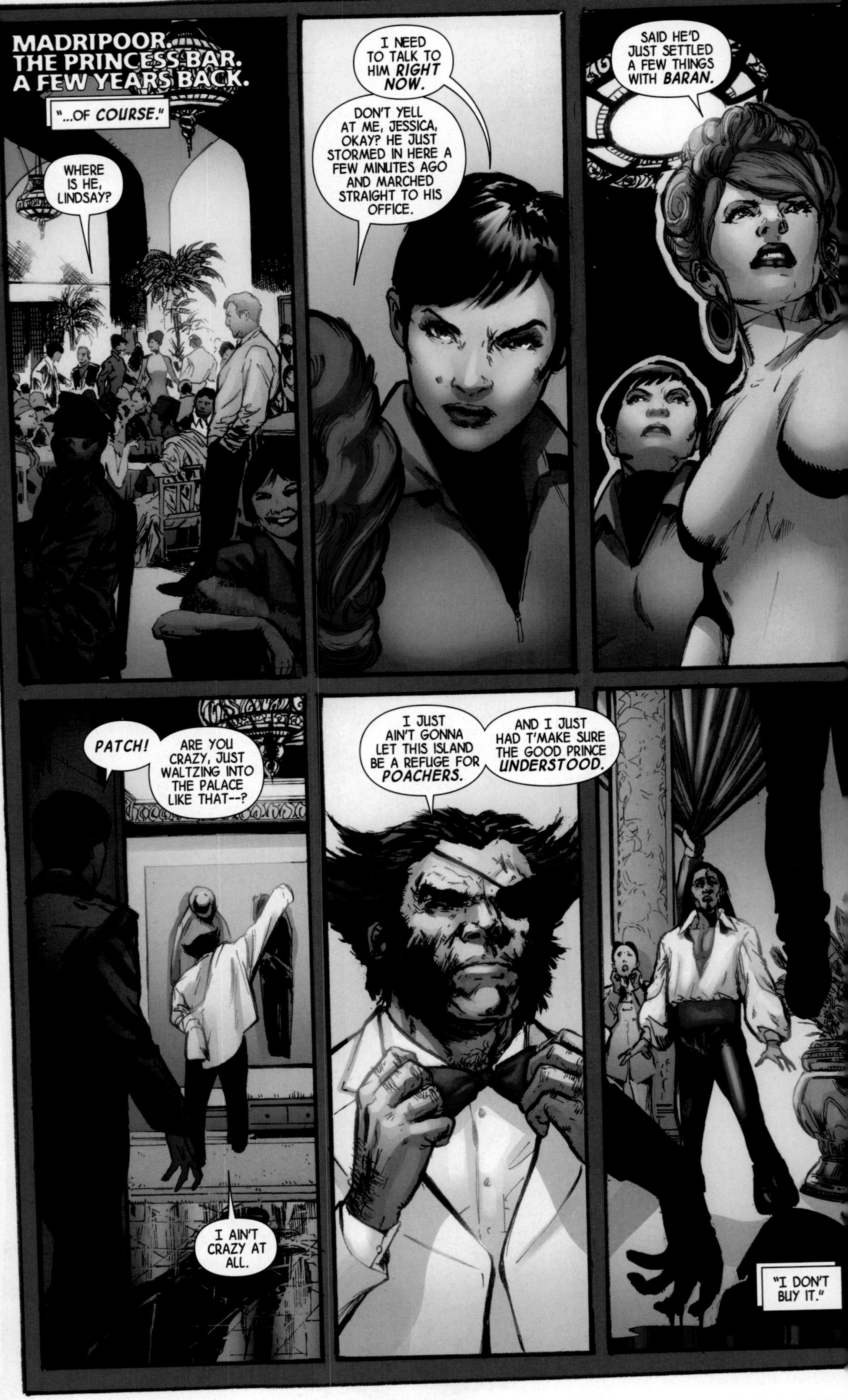

MADRIPOOR. THE PRINCESS BAR. A FEW YEARS BACK.
"...OF COURSE."
WHERE IS HE, LINDSAY?
I NEED TO TALK TO HIM RIGHT NOW.
DON'T YELL AT ME, JESSICA, OKAY? HE JUST STORMED IN HERE A FEW MINUTES AGO AND MARCHED STRAIGHT TO HIS OFFICE.
SAID HE'D JUST SETTLED A FEW THINGS WITH BARAN.
PATCH!
ARE YOU CRAZY, JUST WALTZING INTO THE PALACE LIKE THAT--?
I AIN'T CRAZY AT ALL.
I JUST AIN'T GONNA LET THIS ISLAND BE A REFUGE FOR POACHERS.
AND I JUST HAD T'MAKE SURE THE GOOD PRINCE UNDERSTOOD.
"I DON'T BUY IT."

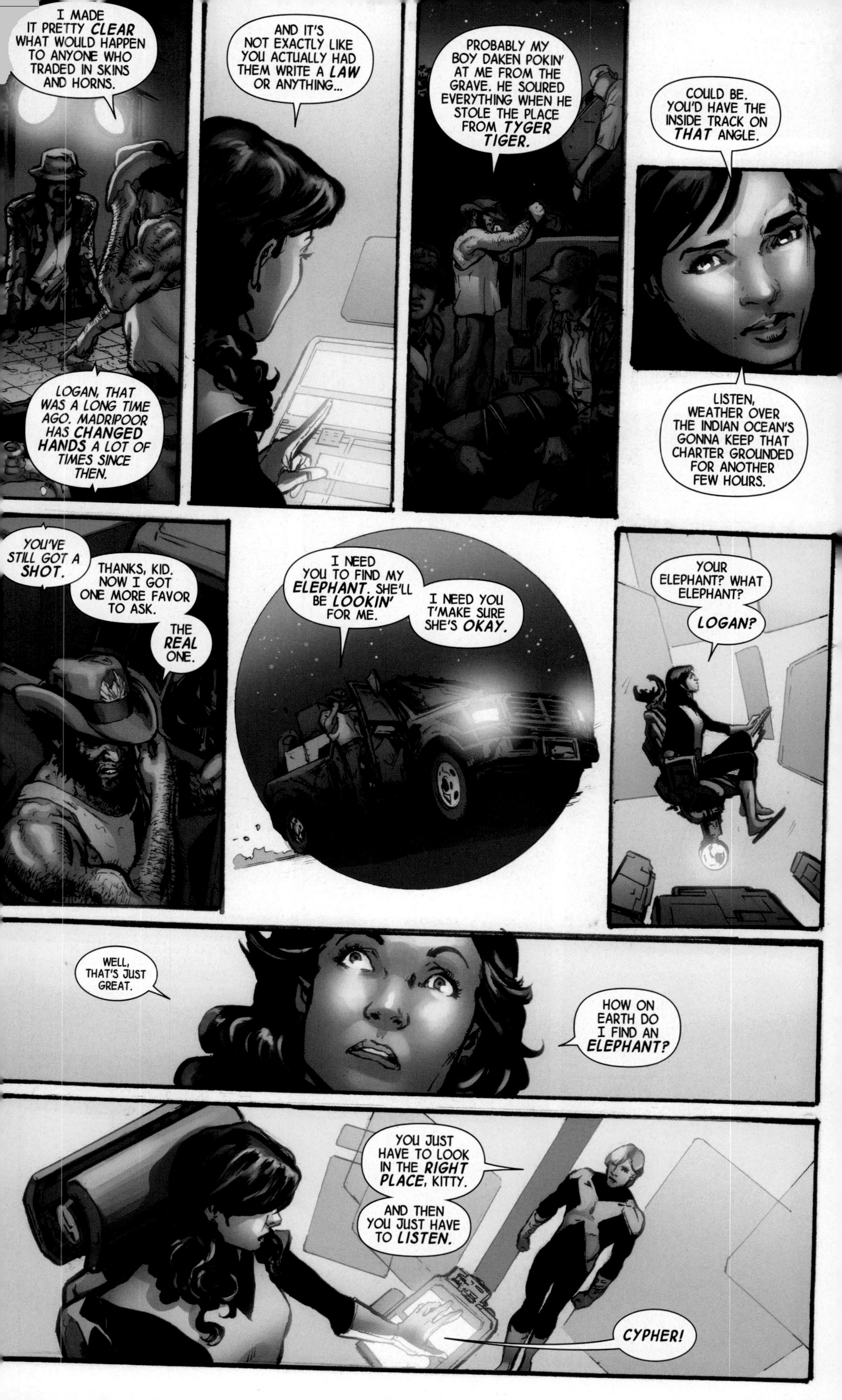

I MADE IT PRETTY CLEAR WHAT WOULD HAPPEN TO ANYONE WHO TRADED IN SKINS AND HORNS.
LOGAN, THAT WAS A LONG TIME AGO. MADRIPOOR HAS CHANGED HANDS A LOT OF TIMES SINCE THEN.
AND IT'S NOT EXACTLY LIKE YOU ACTUALLY HAD THEM WRITE A LAW OR ANYTHING...
PROBABLY MY BOY DAKEN POKIN' AT ME FROM THE GRAVE. HE SOURED EVERYTHING WHEN HE STOLE THE PLACE FROM TYGER TIGER.
COULD BE. YOU'D HAVE THE INSIDE TRACK ON THAT ANGLE.
LISTEN, WEATHER OVER THE INDIAN OCEAN'S GONNA KEEP THAT CHARTER GROUNDED FOR ANOTHER FEW HOURS.
YOU'VE STILL GOT A SHOT.
THANKS, KID. NOW I GOT ONE MORE FAVOR TO ASK.
THE REAL ONE.
I NEED YOU TO FIND MY ELEPHANT. SHE'LL BE LOOKIN' FOR ME.
I NEED YOU T'MAKE SURE SHE'S OKAY.
YOUR ELEPHANT? WHAT ELEPHANT?
LOGAN?
WELL, THAT'S JUST GREAT.
HOW ON EARTH DO I FIND AN ELEPHANT?
YOU JUST HAVE TO LOOK IN THE RIGHT PLACE, KITTY.
AND THEN YOU JUST HAVE TO LISTEN.
CYPHER!

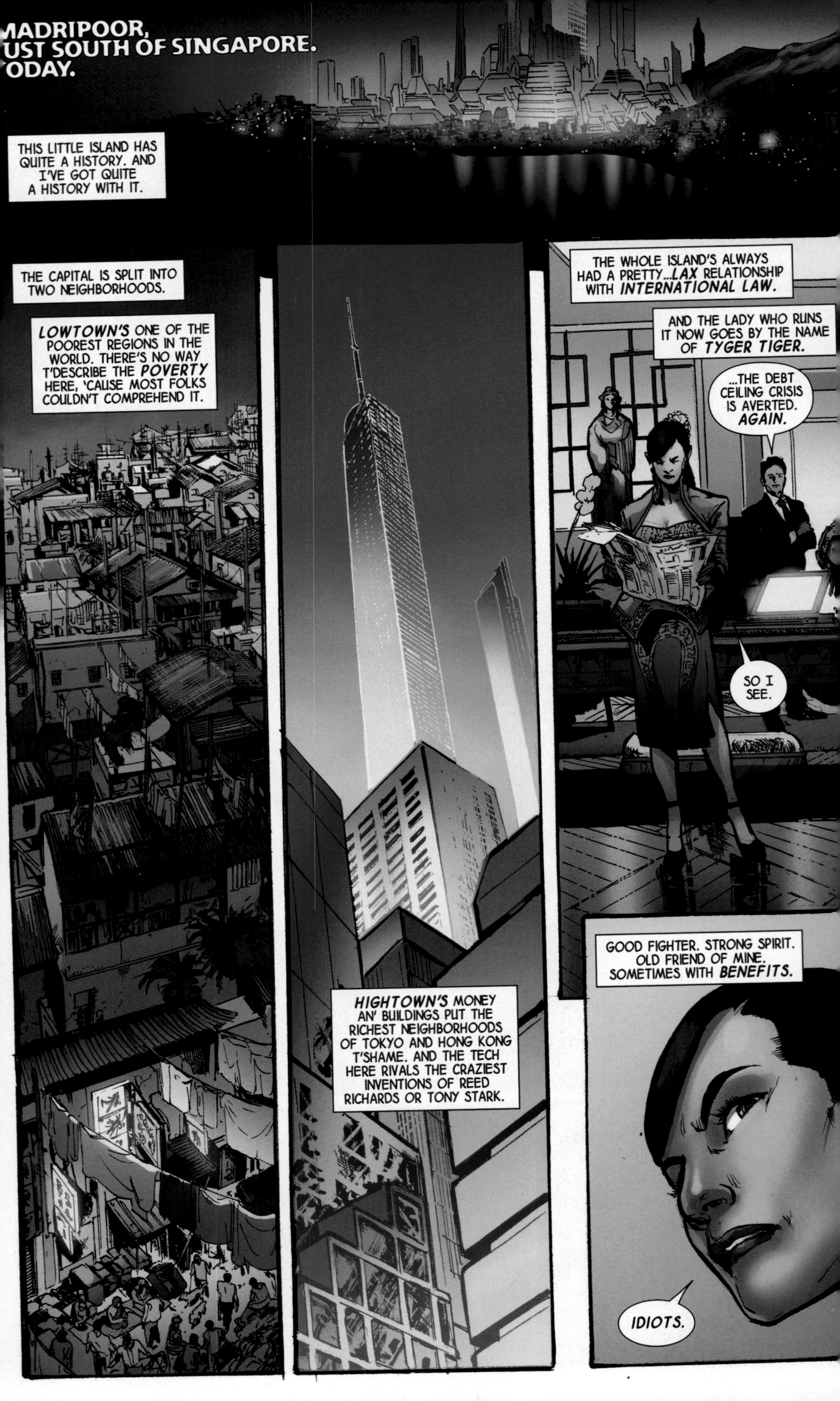

MADRIPOOR, JUST SOUTH OF SINGAPORE. TODAY.
THIS LITTLE ISLAND HAS QUITE A HISTORY. AND I'VE GOT QUITE A HISTORY WITH IT.
THE CAPITAL IS SPLIT INTO TWO NEIGHBORHOODS.
LOWTOWN'S ONE OF THE POOREST REGIONS IN THE WORLD. THERE'S NO WAY T'DESCRIBE THE POVERTY HERE, 'CAUSE MOST FOLKS COULDN'T COMPREHEND IT.
HIGHTOWN'S MONEY AN' BUILDINGS PUT THE RICHEST NEIGHBORHOODS OF TOKYO AND HONG KONG T'SHAME. AND THE TECH HERE RIVALS THE CRAZIEST INVENTIONS OF REED RICHARDS OR TONY STARK.
THE WHOLE ISLAND'S ALWAYS HAD A PRETTY...LAX RELATIONSHIP WITH INTERNATIONAL LAW.
AND THE LADY WHO RUNS IT NOW GOES BY THE NAME OF TYGER TIGER.
...THE DEBT CEILING CRISIS IS AVERTED. AGAIN.
SO I SEE.
GOOD FIGHTER. STRONG SPIRIT. OLD FRIEND OF MINE. SOMETIMES WITH BENEFITS.
IDIOTS.

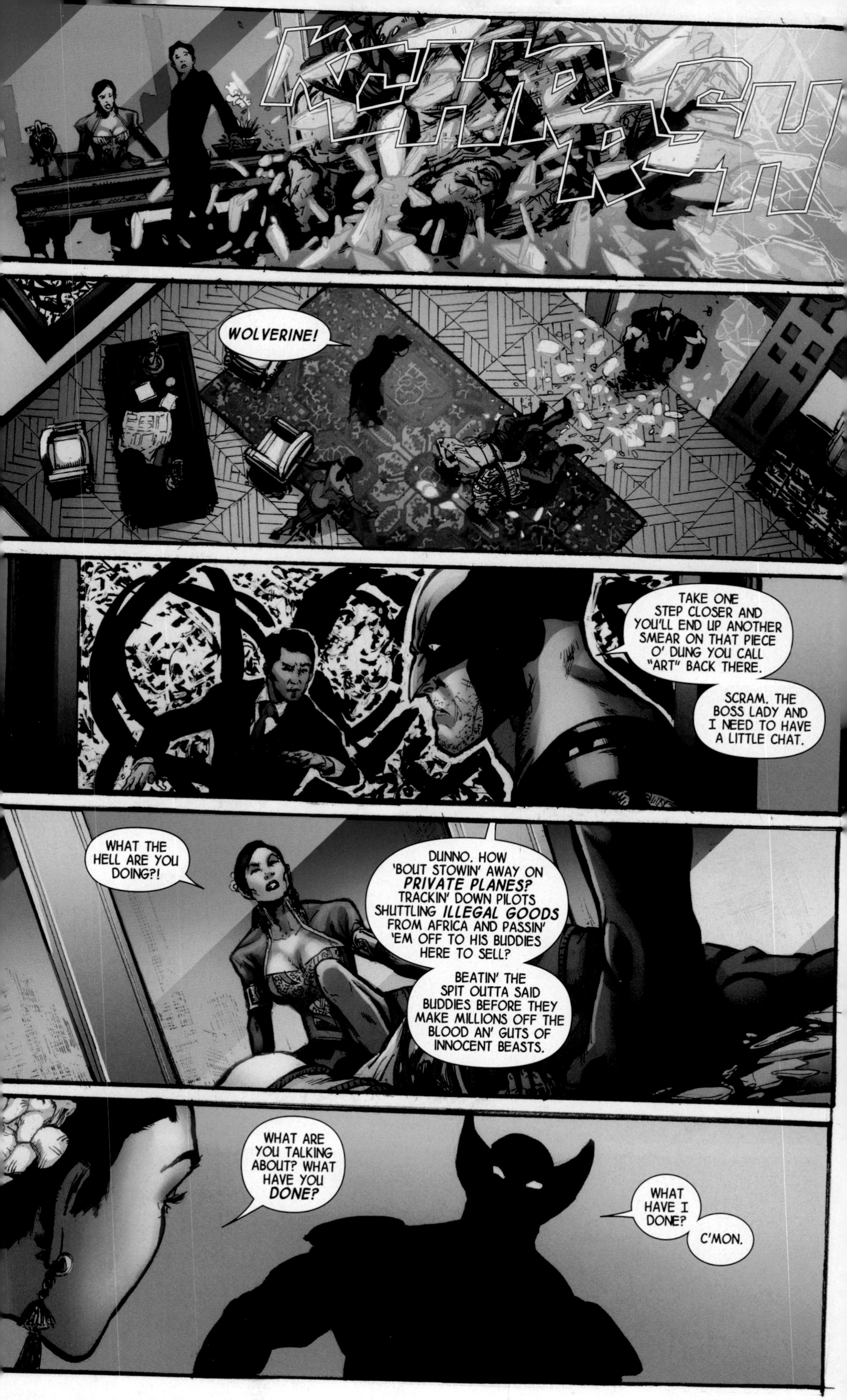
WOLVERINE!
TAKE ONE STEP CLOSER AND YOU'LL END UP ANOTHER SMEAR ON THAT PIECE O' DUNG YOU CALL "ART" BACK THERE.
SCRAM. THE BOSS LADY AND I NEED TO HAVE A LITTLE CHAT.
WHAT THE HELL ARE YOU DOING?!
DUNNO. HOW 'BOUT STOWIN' AWAY ON PRIVATE PLANES? TRACKIN' DOWN PILOTS SHUTTLING ILLEGAL GOODS FROM AFRICA AND PASSIN' 'EM OFF TO HIS BUDDIES HERE TO SELL?
BEATIN' THE SPIT OUTTA SAID BUDDIES BEFORE THEY MAKE MILLIONS OFF THE BLOOD AN' GUTS OF INNOCENT BEASTS.
WHAT ARE YOU TALKING ABOUT? WHAT HAVE YOU DONE?
WHAT HAVE I DONE?
C'MON.

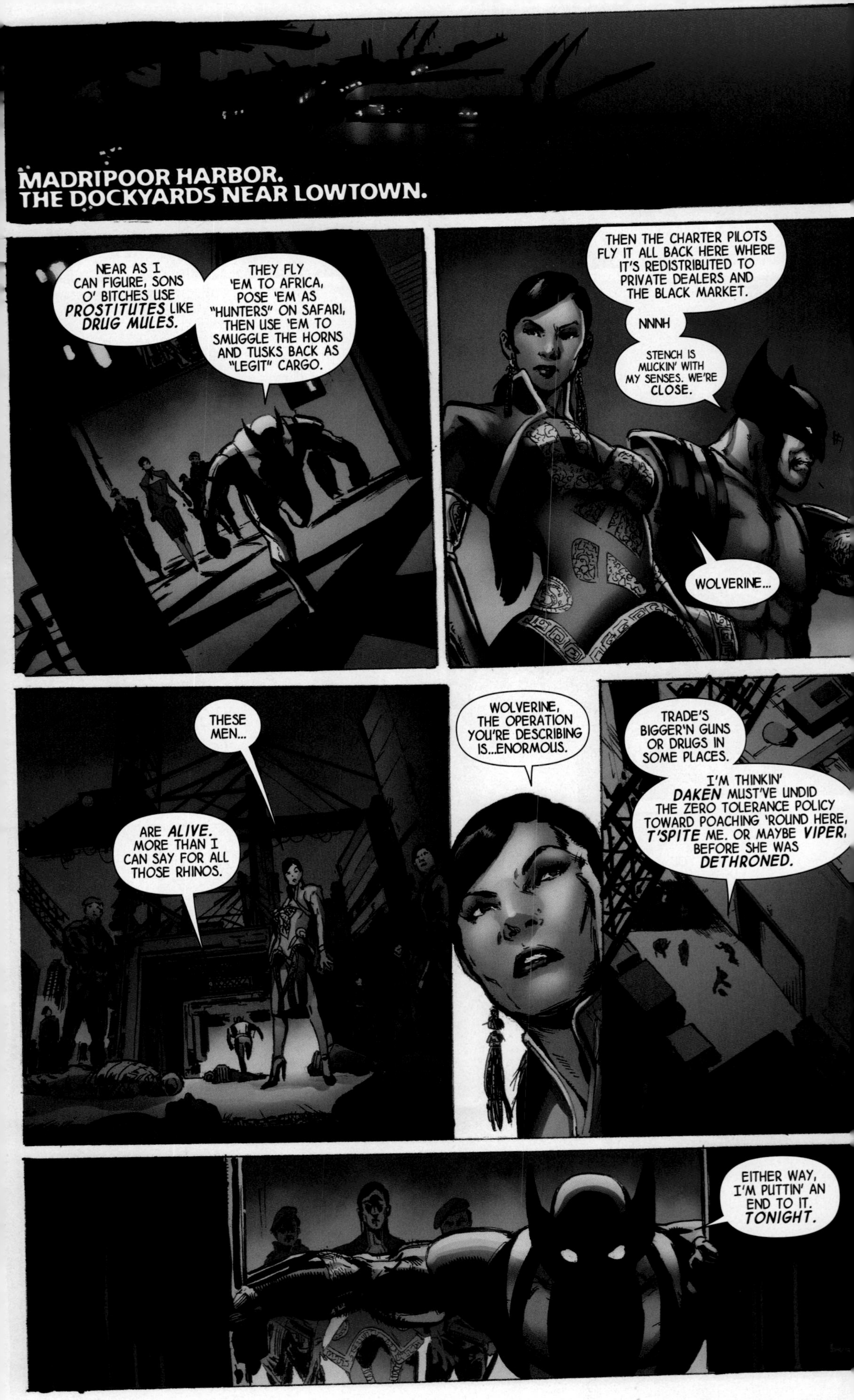
MADRIPOOR HARBOR.
THE DOCKYARDS NEAR LOWTOWN.
NEAR AS I CAN FIGURE, SONS O' BITCHES USE PROSTITUTES LIKE DRUG MULES.
THEY FLY 'EM TO AFRICA, POSE 'EM AS "HUNTERS" ON SAFARI, THEN USE 'EM TO SMUGGLE THE HORNS AND TUSKS BACK AS "LEGIT" CARGO.
THEN THE CHARTER PILOTS FLY IT ALL BACK HERE WHERE IT'S REDISTRIBUTED TO PRIVATE DEALERS AND THE BLACK MARKET.
NNNH
STENCH IS MUCKIN' WITH MY SENSES. WE'RE CLOSE.
WOLVERINE...
THESE MEN...
ARE ALIVE. MORE THAN I CAN SAY FOR ALL THOSE RHINOS.
WOLVERINE, THE OPERATION YOU'RE DESCRIBING IS...ENORMOUS.
TRADE'S BIGGER'N GUNS OR DRUGS IN SOME PLACES.
I'M THINKIN' DAKEN MUST'VE UNDID THE ZERO TOLERANCE POLICY TOWARD POACHING 'ROUND HERE, T'SPITE ME. OR MAYBE VIPER, BEFORE SHE WAS DETHRONED.
EITHER WAY, I'M PUTTIN' AN END TO IT. TONIGHT.

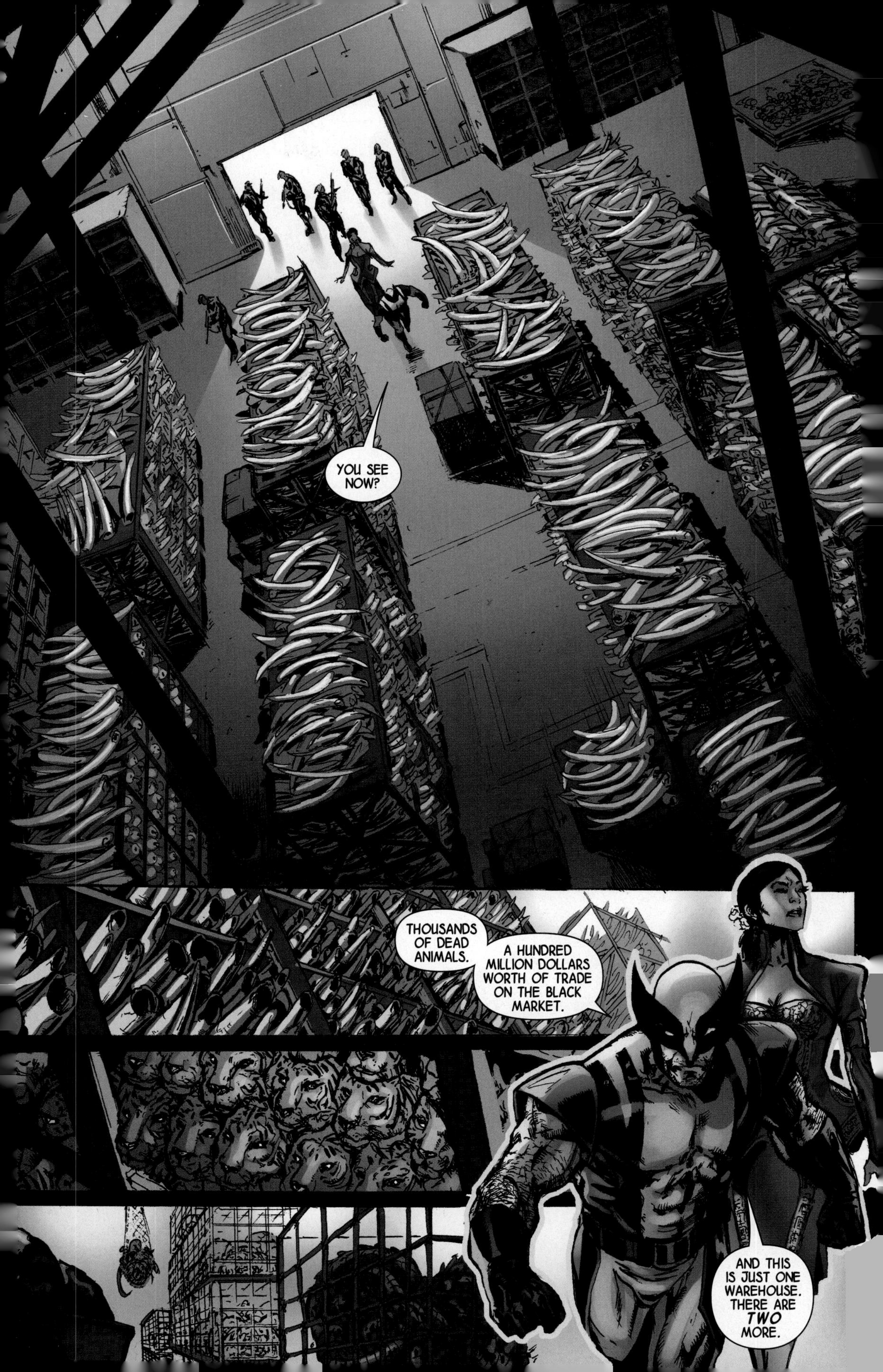
YOU SEE NOW?
THOUSANDS OF DEAD ANIMALS.
A HUNDRED MILLION DOLLARS WORTH OF TRADE ON THE BLACK MARKET.
AND THIS IS JUST ONE WAREHOUSE. THERE ARE TWO MORE.

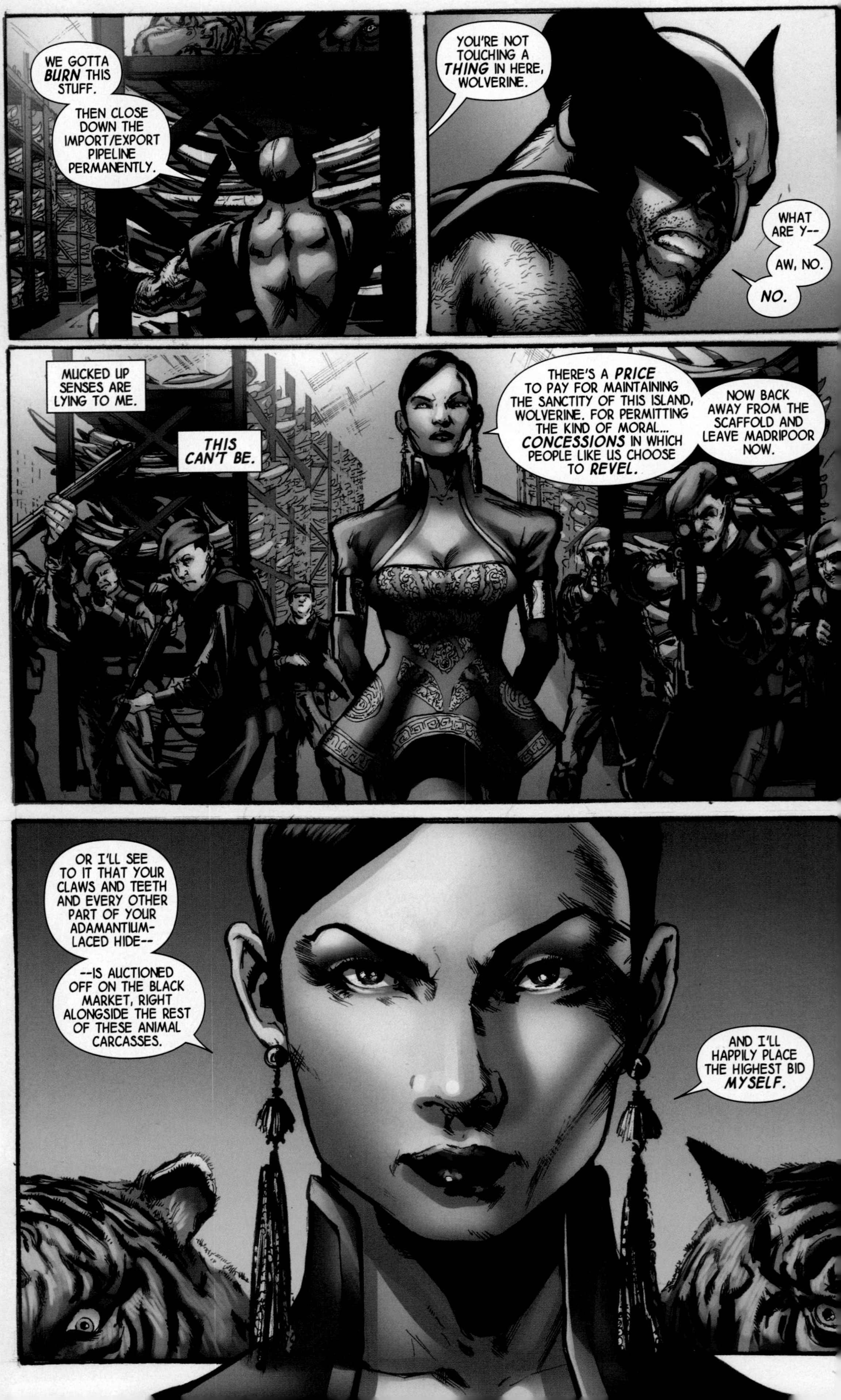
WE GOTTA BURN THIS STUFF.
THEN CLOSE DOWN THE IMPORT/EXPORT PIPELINE PERMANENTLY.
YOU'RE NOT TOUCHING A THING IN HERE, WOLVERINE.
WHAT ARE Y--
AW, NO.
NO.
MUCKED UP SENSES ARE LYING TO ME.
THIS CAN'T BE.
THERE'S A PRICE TO PAY FOR MAINTAINING THE SANCTITY OF THIS ISLAND, WOLVERINE. FOR PERMITTING THE KIND OF MORAL... CONCESSIONS IN WHICH PEOPLE LIKE US CHOOSE TO REVEL.
NOW BACK AWAY FROM THE SCAFFOLD AND LEAVE MADRIPOOR NOW.
OR I'LL SEE TO IT THAT YOUR CLAWS AND TEETH AND EVERY OTHER PART OF YOUR ADAMANTIUM-LACED HIDE--
--IS AUCTIONED OFF ON THE BLACK MARKET, RIGHT ALONGSIDE THE REST OF THESE ANIMAL CARCASSES.
AND I'LL HAPPILY PLACE THE HIGHEST BID MYSELF.

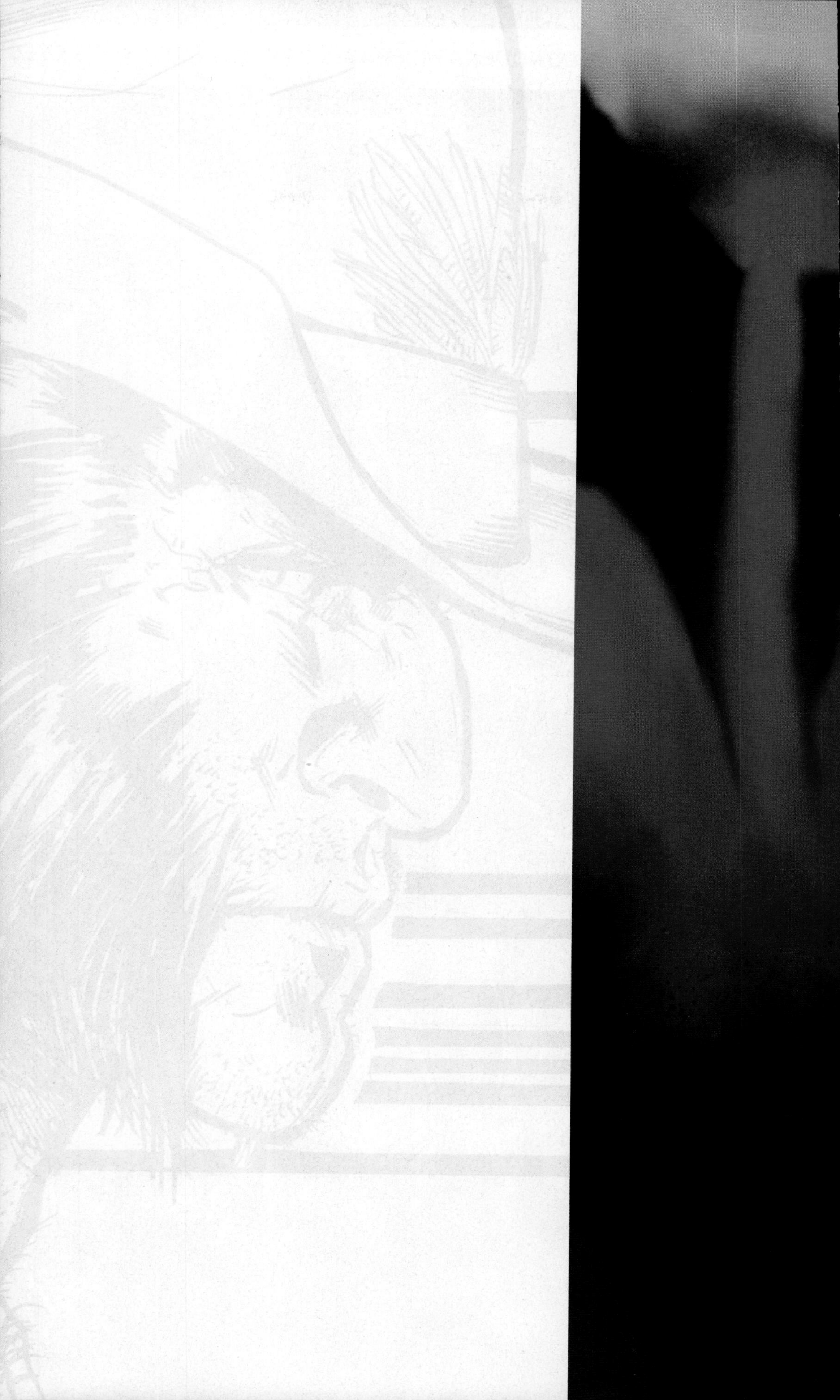

13 COME CONQUER THE BEASTS PART 2: DEATH IN ITS EYES

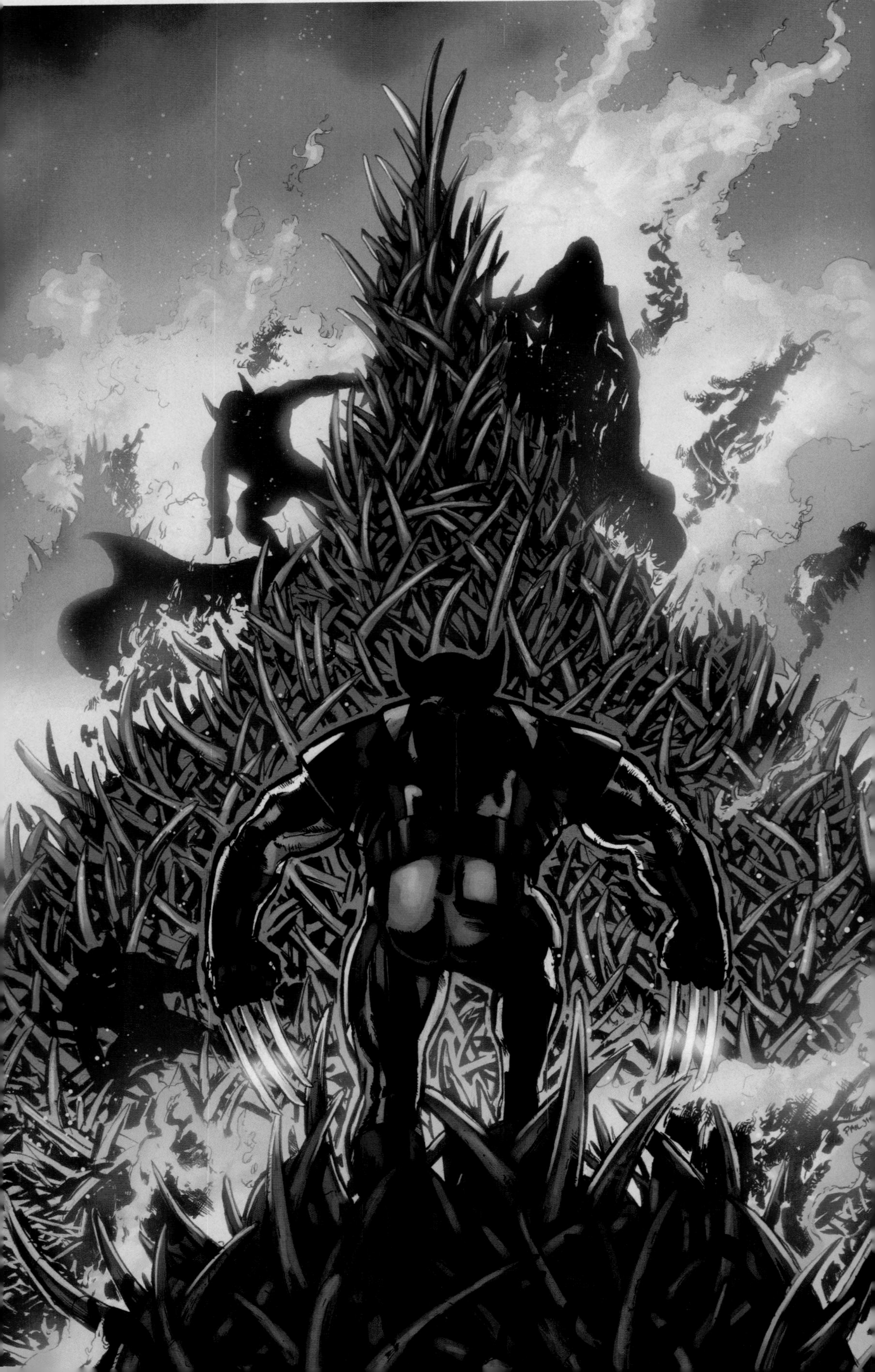

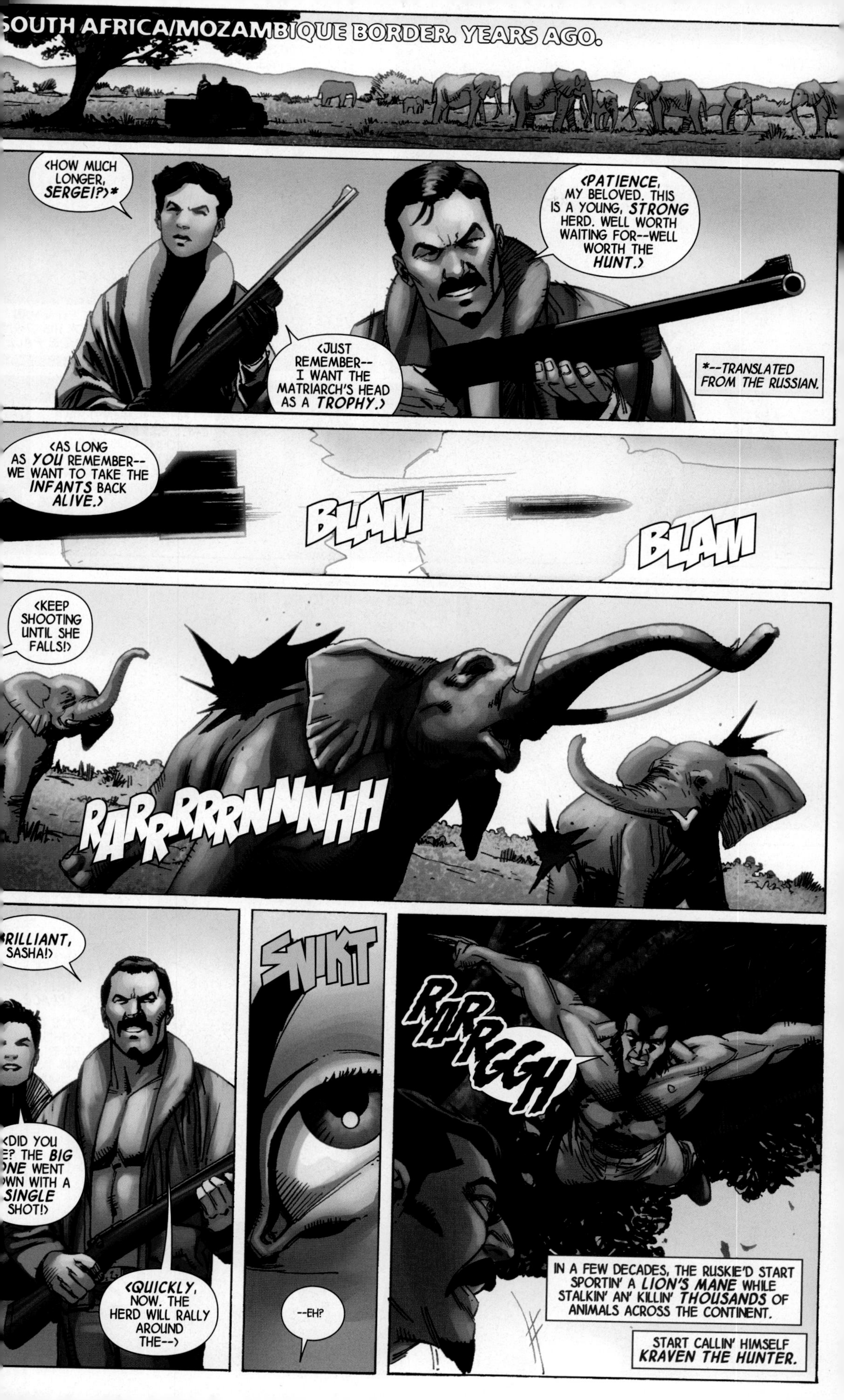
SOUTH AFRICA/MOZAMBIQUE BORDER. YEARS AGO.
<HOW MUCH LONGER, SERGEI?>*
<PATIENCE, MY BELOVED. THIS IS A YOUNG, STRONG HERD. WELL WORTH WAITING FOR--WELL WORTH THE HUNT.>
<JUST REMEMBER-- I WANT THE MATRIARCH'S HEAD AS A TROPHY.>
*--TRANSLATED FROM THE RUSSIAN.
<AS LONG AS YOU REMEMBER-- WE WANT TO TAKE THE INFANTS BACK ALIVE.>
BLAM
BLAM
<KEEP SHOOTING UNTIL SHE FALLS!>
RARRRRRNNNHH
RILLIANT, SASHA!>
<DID YOU E? THE BIG NE WENT WN WITH A SINGLE SHOT!>
<QUICKLY, NOW. THE HERD WILL RALLY AROUND THE-->
SNIKT
--EH?
RARRGGH
IN A FEW DECADES, THE RUSKIE'D START SPORTIN' A LION'S MANE WHILE STALKIN' AN' KILLIN' THOUSANDS OF ANIMALS ACROSS THE CONTINENT.
START CALLIN' HIMSELF KRAVEN THE HUNTER.

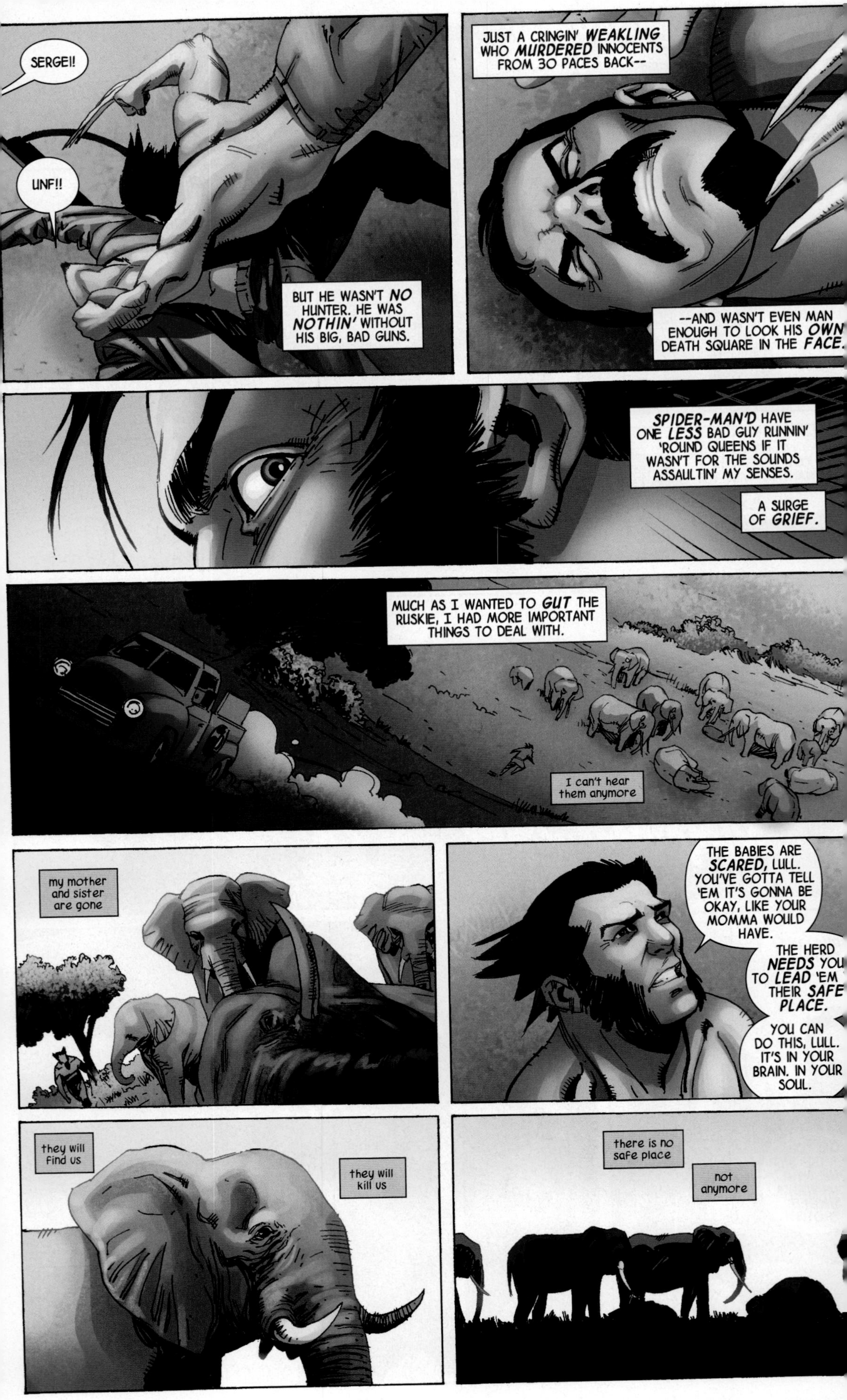
SERGEI!
UNF!!
BUT HE WASN'T NO HUNTER. HE WAS NOTHIN' WITHOUT HIS BIG, BAD GUNS.
JUST A CRINGIN' WEAKLING WHO MURDERED INNOCENTS FROM 30 PACES BACK--
--AND WASN'T EVEN MAN ENOUGH TO LOOK HIS OWN DEATH SQUARE IN THE FACE.
SPIDER-MAN'D HAVE ONE LESS BAD GUY RUNNIN' 'ROUND QUEENS IF IT WASN'T FOR THE SOUNDS ASSAULTIN' MY SENSES.
A SURGE OF GRIEF.
MUCH AS I WANTED TO GUT THE RUSKIE, I HAD MORE IMPORTANT THINGS TO DEAL WITH.
I can't hear them anymore
my mother and sister are gone
THE BABIES ARE SCARED, LULL. YOU'VE GOTTA TELL 'EM IT'S GONNA BE OKAY, LIKE YOUR MOMMA WOULD HAVE.
THE HERD NEEDS YOU TO LEAD 'EM THEIR SAFE PLACE.
YOU CAN DO THIS, LULL. IT'S IN YOUR BRAIN. IN YOUR SOUL.
they will find us
they will kill us
there is no safe place
not anymore

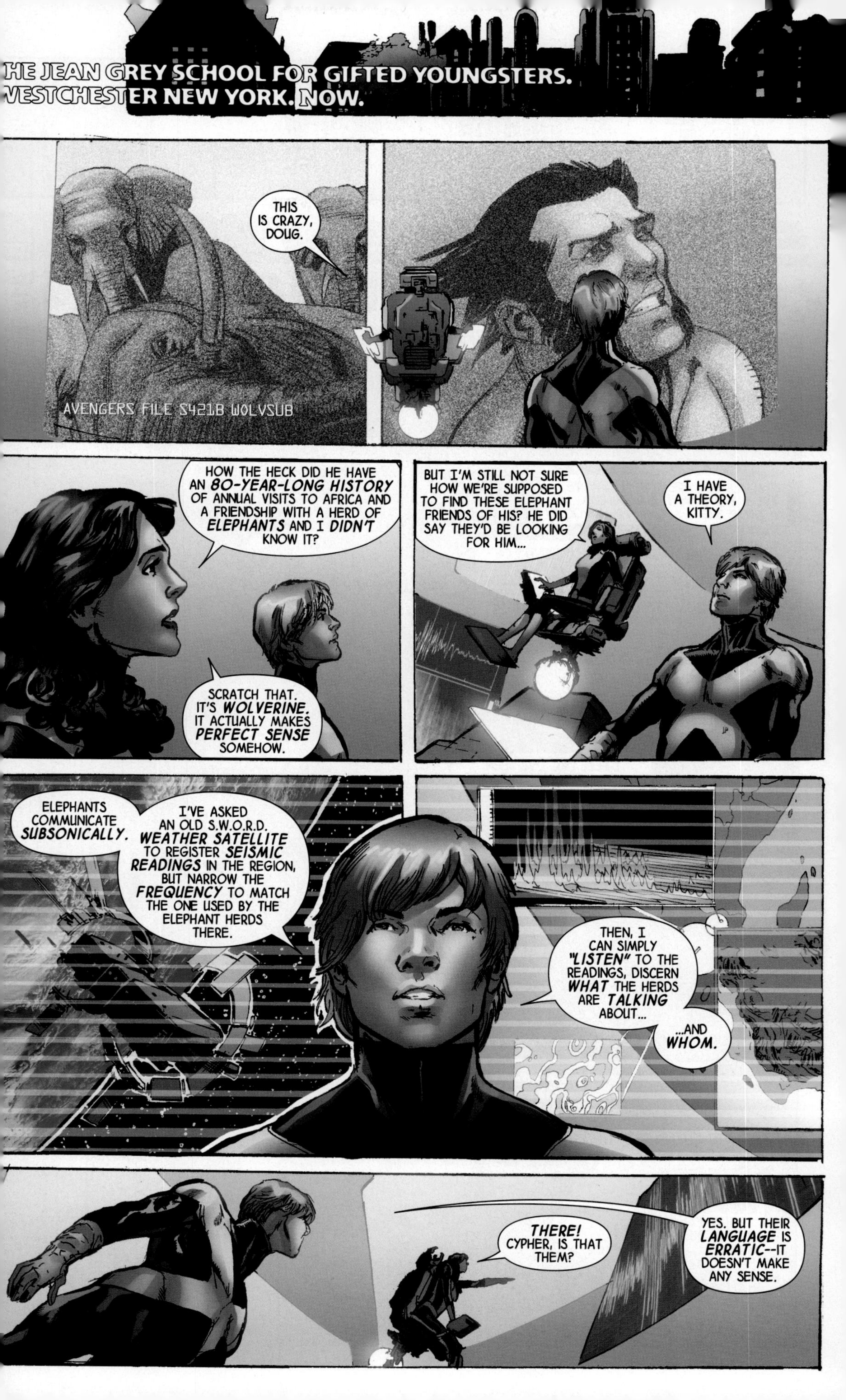

HE JEAN GREY SCHOOL FOR GIFTED YOUNGSTERS.
VESTCHESTER NEW YORK. NOW.
THIS IS CRAZY, DOUG.
AVENGERS FILE S421B WOLVSUB
HOW THE HECK DID HE HAVE AN 80-YEAR-LONG HISTORY OF ANNUAL VISITS TO AFRICA AND A FRIENDSHIP WITH A HERD OF ELEPHANTS AND I DIDN'T KNOW IT?
SCRATCH THAT. IT'S WOLVERINE. IT ACTUALLY MAKES PERFECT SENSE SOMEHOW.
BUT I'M STILL NOT SURE HOW WE'RE SUPPOSED TO FIND THESE ELEPHANT FRIENDS OF HIS? HE DID SAY THEY'D BE LOOKING FOR HIM...
I HAVE A THEORY, KITTY.
ELEPHANTS COMMUNICATE SUBSONICALLY.
I'VE ASKED AN OLD S.W.O.R.D. WEATHER SATELLITE TO REGISTER SEISMIC READINGS IN THE REGION, BUT NARROW THE FREQUENCY TO MATCH THE ONE USED BY THE ELEPHANT HERDS THERE.
THEN, I CAN SIMPLY "LISTEN" TO THE READINGS, DISCERN WHAT THE HERDS ARE TALKING ABOUT...
...AND WHOM.
THERE! CYPHER, IS THAT THEM?
YES. BUT THEIR LANGUAGE IS ERRATIC--IT DOESN'T MAKE ANY SENSE.

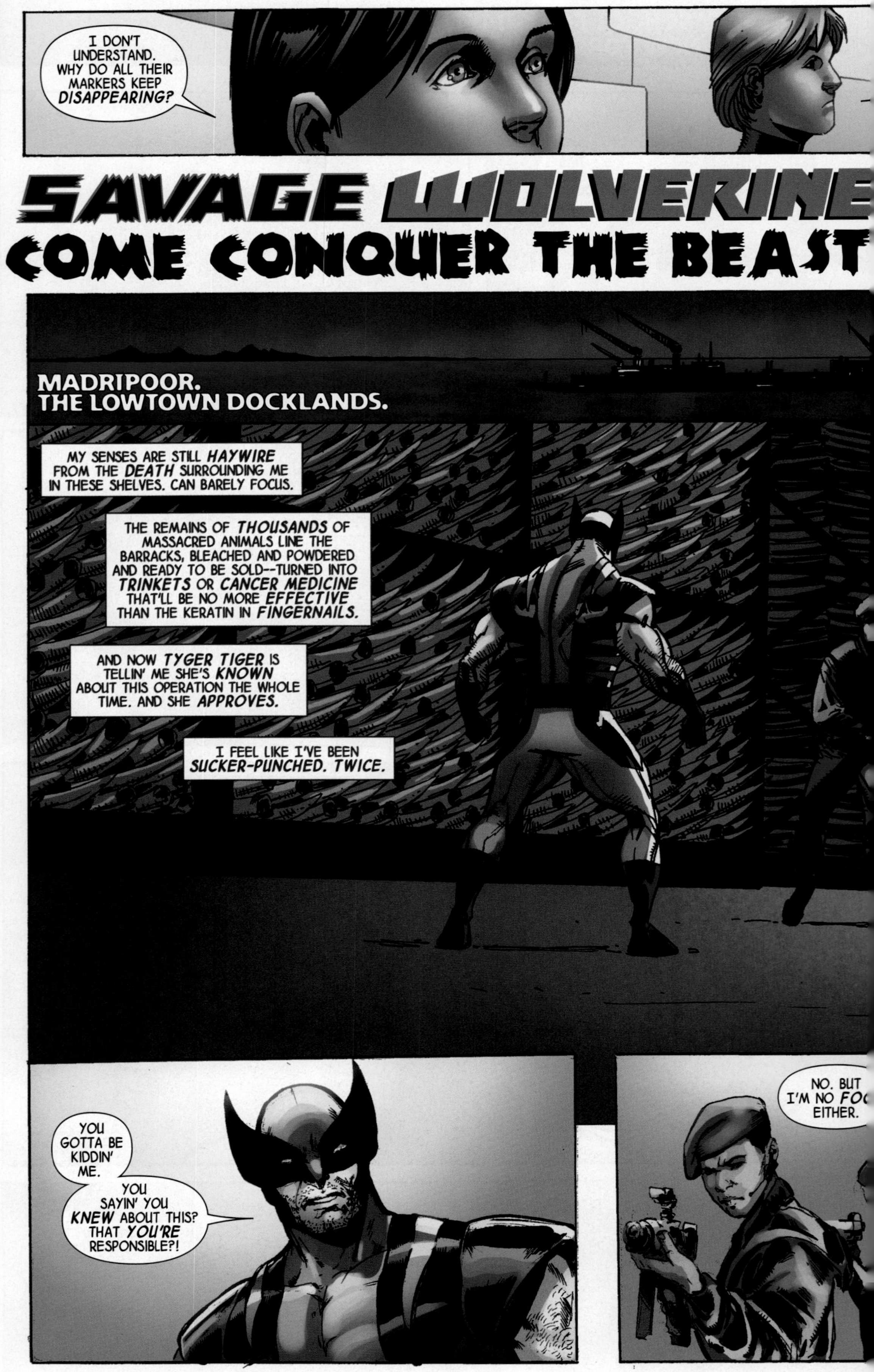

I DON'T UNDERSTAND. WHY DO ALL THEIR MARKERS KEEP DISAPPEARING?
SAVAGE WOLVERINE
COME CONQUER THE BEAST
MADRIPOOR. THE LOWTOWN DOCKLANDS.
MY SENSES ARE STILL HAYWIRE FROM THE DEATH SURROUNDING ME IN THESE SHELVES. CAN BARELY FOCUS.
THE REMAINS OF THOUSANDS OF MASSACRED ANIMALS LINE THE BARRACKS, BLEACHED AND POWDERED AND READY TO BE SOLD--TURNED INTO TRINKETS OR CANCER MEDICINE THAT'LL BE NO MORE EFFECTIVE THAN THE KERATIN IN FINGERNAILS.
AND NOW TYGER TIGER IS TELLIN' ME SHE'S KNOWN ABOUT THIS OPERATION THE WHOLE TIME. AND SHE APPROVES.
I FEEL LIKE I'VE BEEN SUCKER-PUNCHED. TWICE.
YOU GOTTA BE KIDDIN' ME.
YOU SAYIN' YOU KNEW ABOUT THIS? THAT YOU'RE RESPONSIBLE?!
NO. BUT I'M NO FO
EITHER.

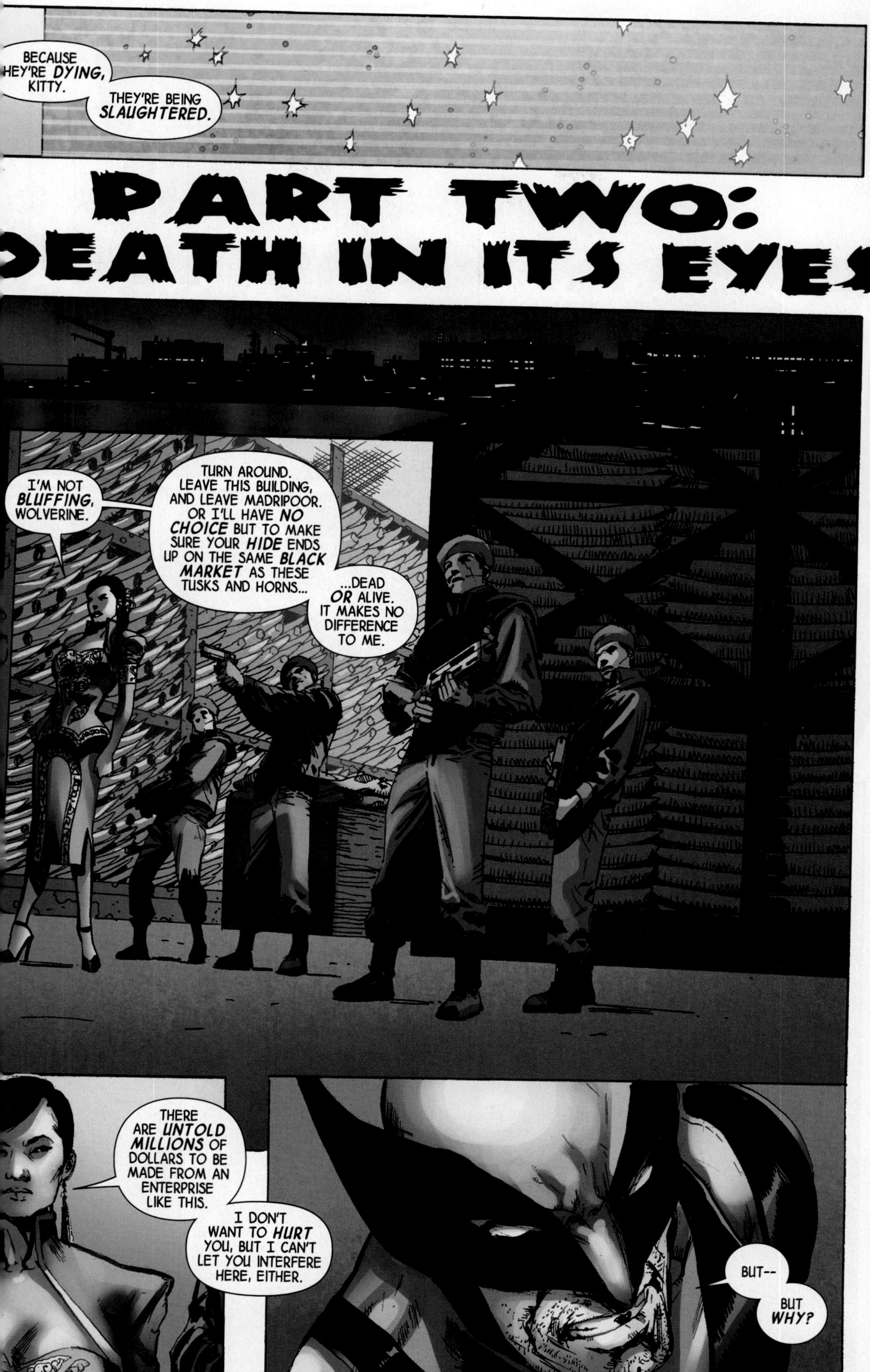

BECAUSE HEY'RE DYING, KITTY.
THEY'RE BEING SLAUGHTERED.
PART TWO: EATH IN ITS EYES
I'M NOT BLUFFING, WOLVERINE.
TURN AROUND. LEAVE THIS BUILDING, AND LEAVE MADRIPOOR. OR I'LL HAVE NO CHOICE BUT TO MAKE SURE YOUR HIDE ENDS UP ON THE SAME BLACK MARKET AS THESE TUSKS AND HORNS...
...DEAD OR ALIVE. IT MAKES NO DIFFERENCE TO ME.
THERE ARE UNTOLD MILLIONS OF DOLLARS TO BE MADE FROM AN ENTERPRISE LIKE THIS.
I DON'T WANT TO HURT YOU, BUT I CAN'T LET YOU INTERFERE HERE, EITHER.
BUT--
BUT WHY?

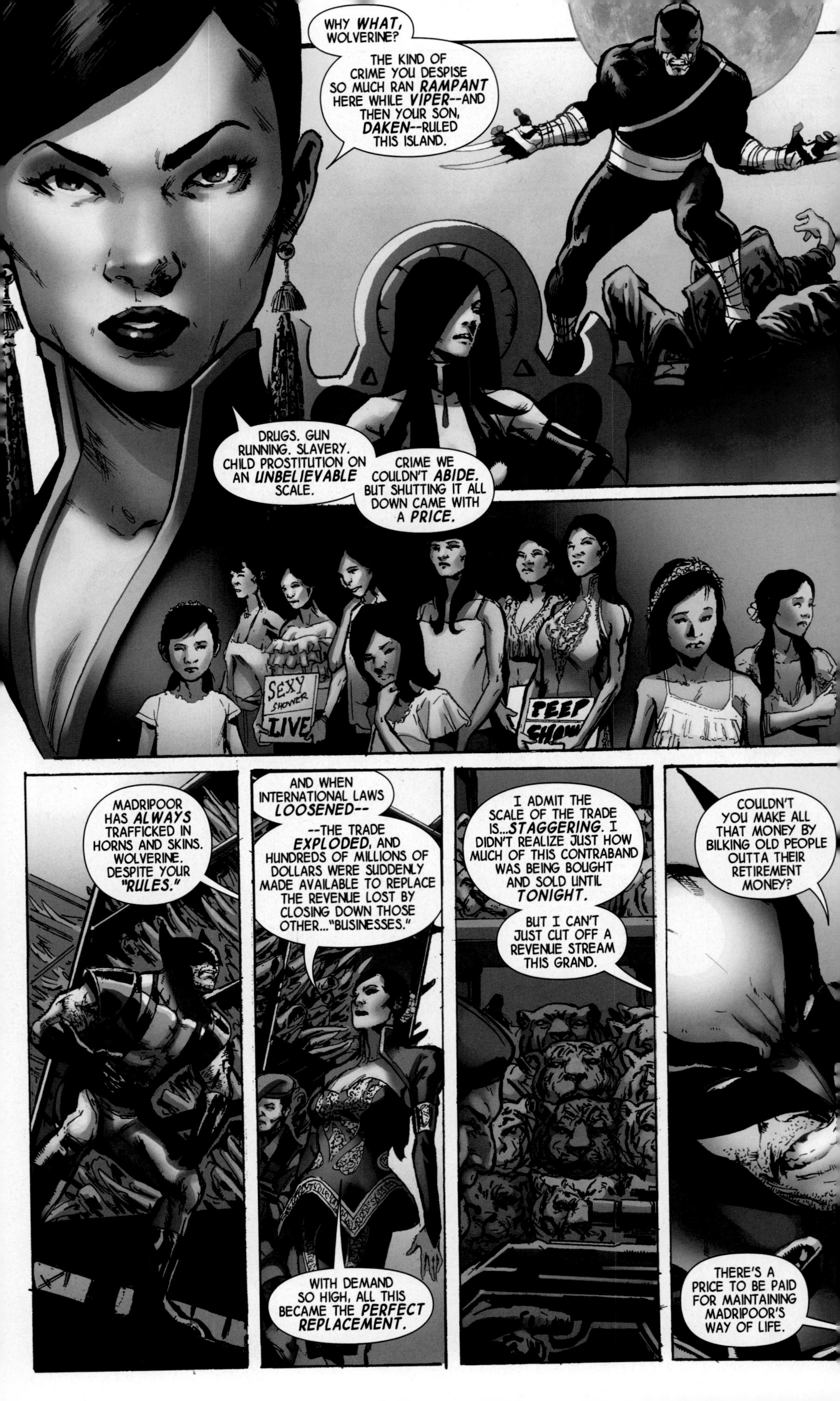
WHY WHAT, WOLVERINE?
THE KIND OF CRIME YOU DESPISE SO MUCH RAN RAMPANT HERE WHILE VIPER--AND THEN YOUR SON, DAKEN--RULED THIS ISLAND.
DRUGS. GUN RUNNING. SLAVERY. CHILD PROSTITUTION ON AN UNBELIEVABLE SCALE.
CRIME WE COULDN'T ABIDE. BUT SHUTTING IT ALL DOWN CAME WITH A PRICE.
SEXY SHOWER LIVE
PEEP SHOW
MADRIPOOR HAS ALWAYS TRAFFICKED IN HORNS AND SKINS. WOLVERINE. DESPITE YOUR "RULES."
AND WHEN INTERNATIONAL LAWS LOOSENED--
--THE TRADE EXPLODED, AND HUNDREDS OF MILLIONS OF DOLLARS WERE SUDDENLY MADE AVAILABLE TO REPLACE THE REVENUE LOST BY CLOSING DOWN THOSE OTHER..."BUSINESSES."
WITH DEMAND SO HIGH, ALL THIS BECAME THE PERFECT REPLACEMENT.
I ADMIT THE SCALE OF THE TRADE IS...STAGGERING. I DIDN'T REALIZE JUST HOW MUCH OF THIS CONTRABAND WAS BEING BOUGHT AND SOLD UNTIL TONIGHT.
BUT I CAN'T JUST CUT OFF A REVENUE STREAM THIS GRAND.
COULDN'T YOU MAKE ALL THAT MONEY BY BILKING OLD PEOPLE OUTTA THEIR RETIREMENT MONEY?
THERE'S A PRICE TO BE PAID FOR MAINTAINING MADRIPOOR'S WAY OF LIFE.

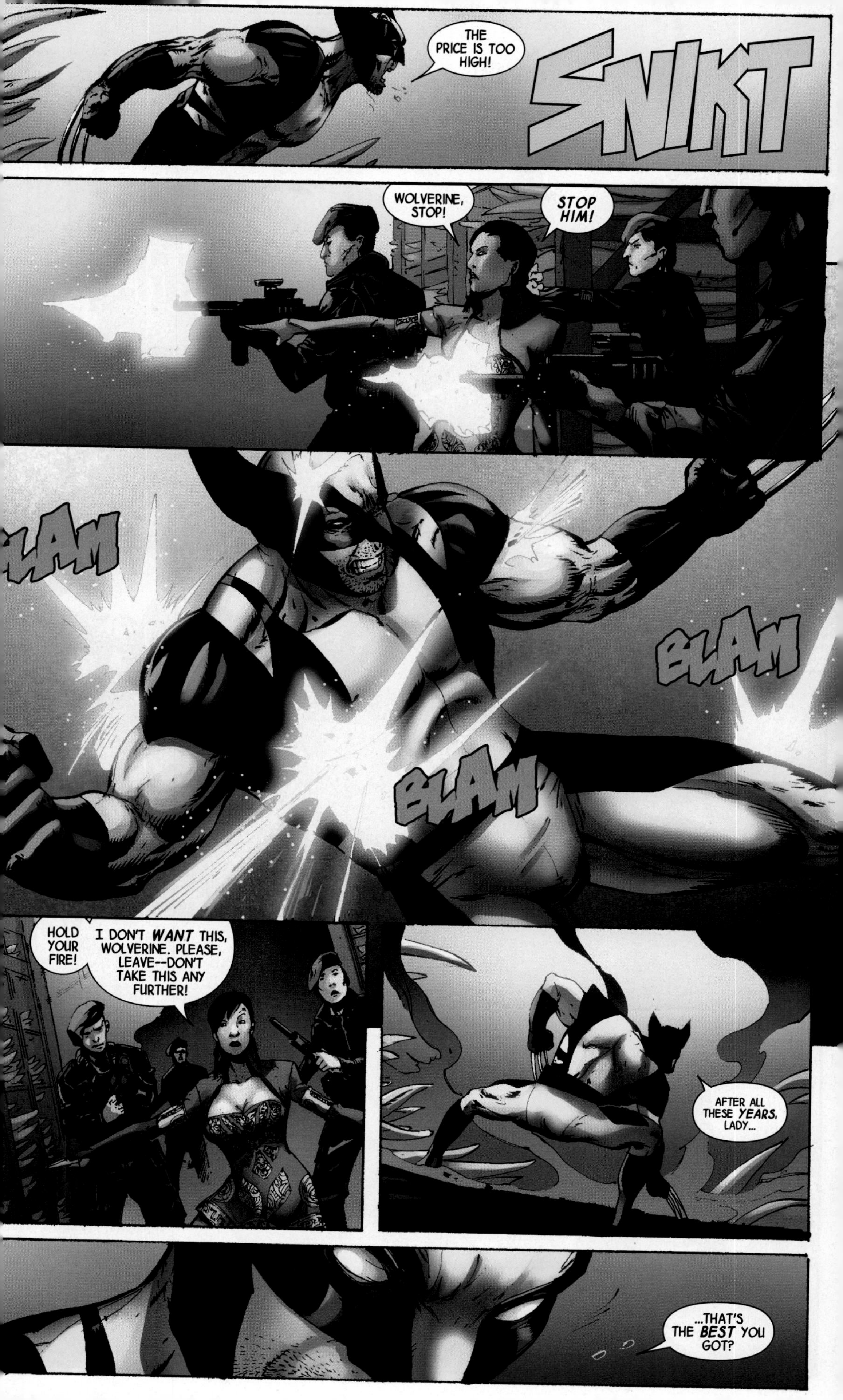
THE PRICE IS TOO HIGH!
SNIKT
WOLVERINE, STOP!
STOP HIM!
BLAM
BLAM
BLAM
HOLD YOUR FIRE!
I DON'T WANT THIS, WOLVERINE. PLEASE, LEAVE--DON'T TAKE THIS ANY FURTHER!
AFTER ALL THESE YEARS, LADY...
...THAT'S THE BEST YOU GOT?

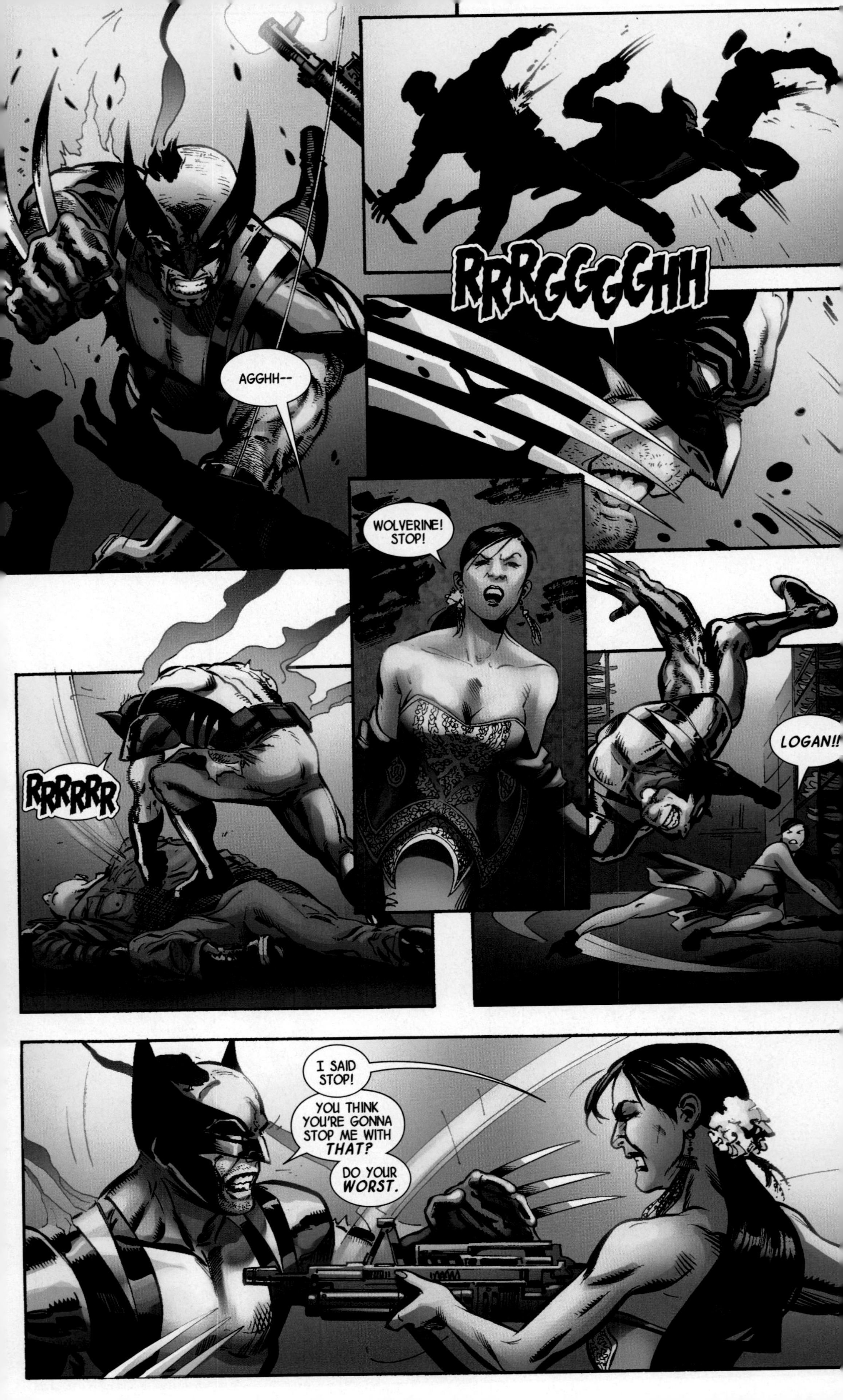

AGGHH--
RRRGGGGHH
WOLVERINE! STOP!
RRRRRR
LOGAN!!
I SAID STOP!
YOU THINK YOU'RE GONNA STOP ME WITH THAT?
DO YOUR WORST.

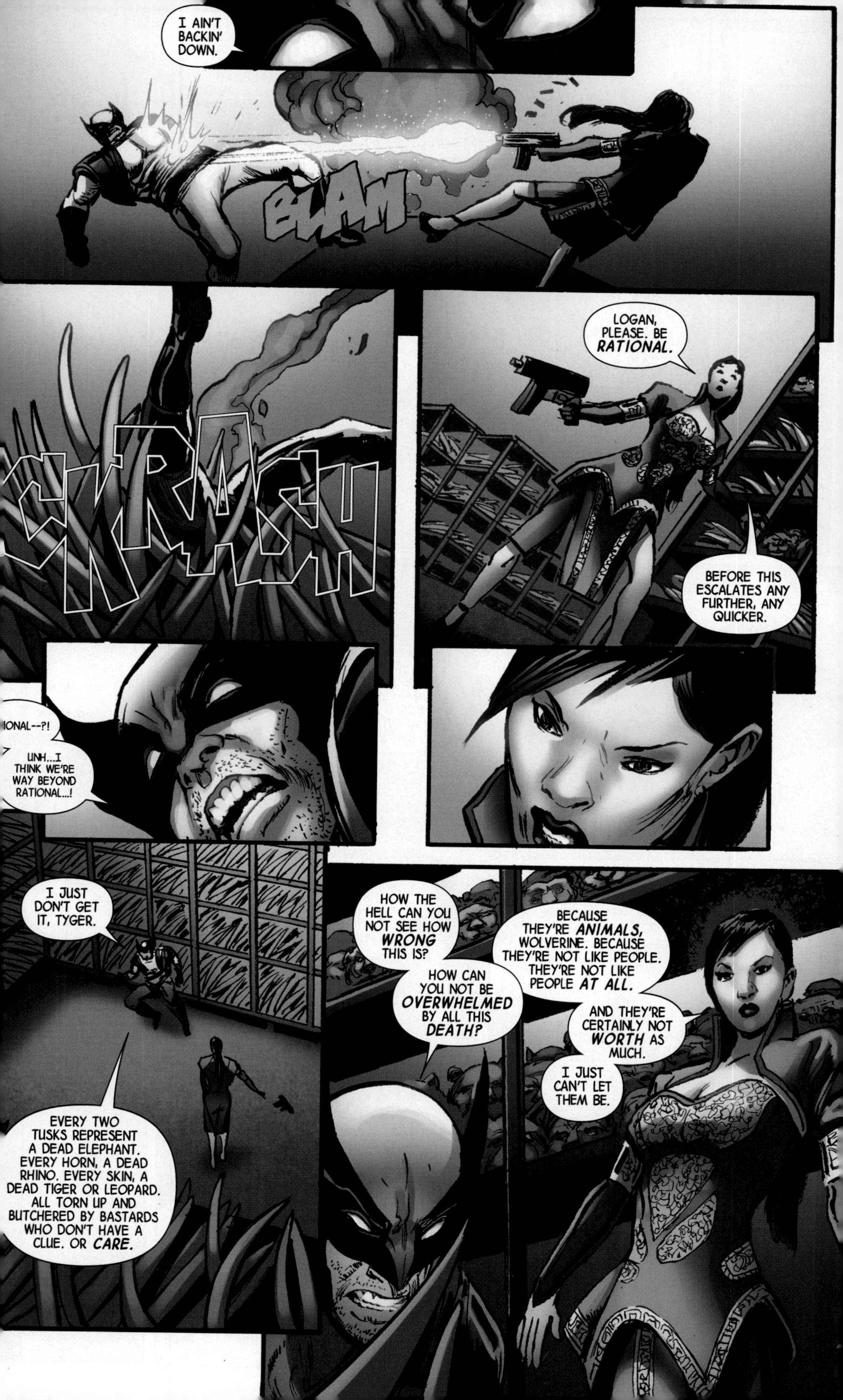

I AIN'T BACKIN' DOWN.
BLAM
CKRASH
LOGAN, PLEASE. BE RATIONAL.
BEFORE THIS ESCALATES ANY FURTHER, ANY QUICKER.
IONAL--?!
UNH...I THINK WE'RE WAY BEYOND RATIONAL...!
I JUST DON'T GET IT, TYGER.
EVERY TWO TUSKS REPRESENT A DEAD ELEPHANT. EVERY HORN, A DEAD RHINO. EVERY SKIN, A DEAD TIGER OR LEOPARD. ALL TORN UP AND BUTCHERED BY BASTARDS WHO DON'T HAVE A CLUE. OR CARE.
HOW THE HELL CAN YOU NOT SEE HOW WRONG THIS IS?
HOW CAN YOU NOT BE OVERWHELMED BY ALL THIS DEATH?
BECAUSE THEY'RE ANIMALS, WOLVERINE. BECAUSE THEY'RE NOT LIKE PEOPLE. THEY'RE NOT LIKE PEOPLE AT ALL.
AND THEY'RE CERTAINLY NOT WORTH AS MUCH.
I JUST CAN'T LET THEM BE.

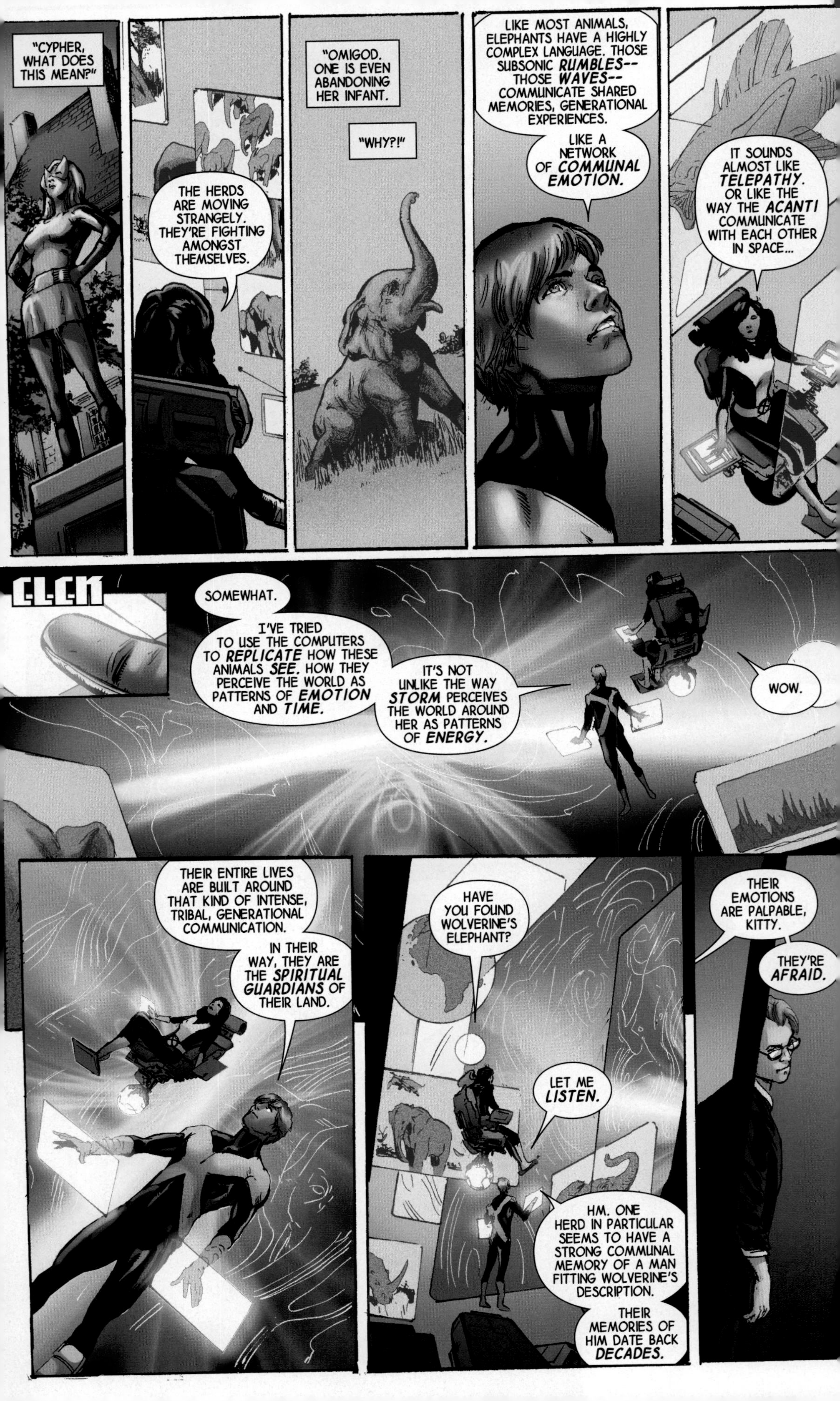
"CYPHER, WHAT DOES THIS MEAN?"
THE HERDS ARE MOVING STRANGELY. THEY'RE FIGHTING AMONGST THEMSELVES.
"OMIGOD. ONE IS EVEN ABANDONING HER INFANT.
"WHY?!"
LIKE MOST ANIMALS, ELEPHANTS HAVE A HIGHLY COMPLEX LANGUAGE. THOSE SUBSONIC RUMBLES-- THOSE WAVES-- COMMUNICATE SHARED MEMORIES, GENERATIONAL EXPERIENCES.
LIKE A NETWORK OF COMMUNAL EMOTION.
IT SOUNDS ALMOST LIKE TELEPATHY. OR LIKE THE WAY THE ACANTI COMMUNICATE WITH EACH OTHER IN SPACE...
CLCK
SOMEWHAT.
I'VE TRIED TO USE THE COMPUTERS TO REPLICATE HOW THESE ANIMALS SEE. HOW THEY PERCEIVE THE WORLD AS PATTERNS OF EMOTION AND TIME.
IT'S NOT UNLIKE THE WAY STORM PERCEIVES THE WORLD AROUND HER AS PATTERNS OF ENERGY.
WOW.
THEIR ENTIRE LIVES ARE BUILT AROUND THAT KIND OF INTENSE, TRIBAL, GENERATIONAL COMMUNICATION.
IN THEIR WAY, THEY ARE THE SPIRITUAL GUARDIANS OF THEIR LAND.
HAVE YOU FOUND WOLVERINE'S ELEPHANT?
LET ME LISTEN.
HM. ONE HERD IN PARTICULAR SEEMS TO HAVE A STRONG COMMUNAL MEMORY OF A MAN FITTING WOLVERINE'S DESCRIPTION.
THEIR MEMORIES OF HIM DATE BACK DECADES.
THEIR EMOTIONS ARE PALPABLE, KITTY.
THEY'RE AFRAID.

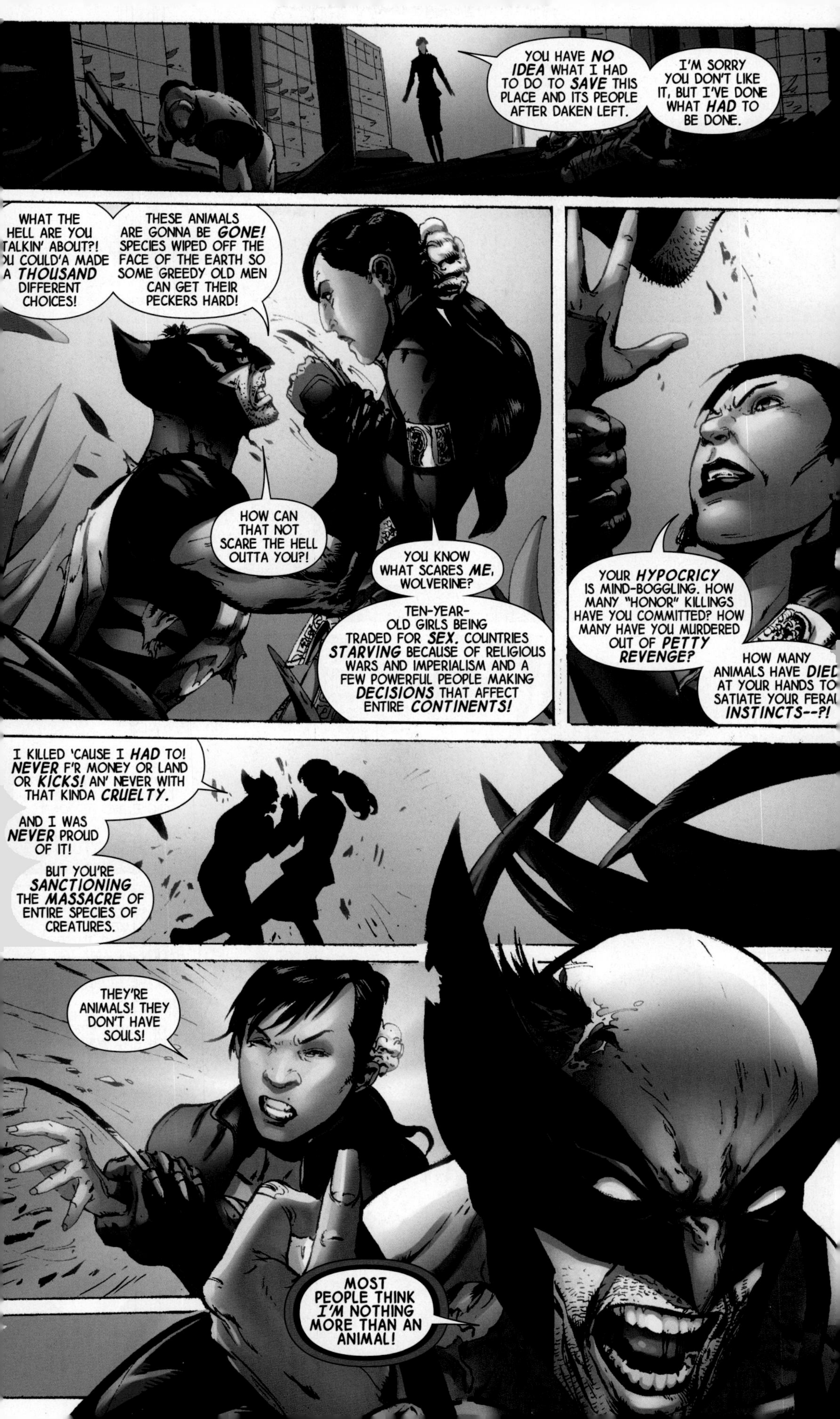

YOU HAVE NO IDEA WHAT I HAD TO DO TO SAVE THIS PLACE AND ITS PEOPLE AFTER DAKEN LEFT.
I'M SORRY YOU DON'T LIKE IT, BUT I'VE DONE WHAT HAD TO BE DONE.
WHAT THE HELL ARE YOU TALKIN' ABOUT?! OU COULD'A MADE A THOUSAND DIFFERENT CHOICES!
THESE ANIMALS ARE GONNA BE GONE! SPECIES WIPED OFF THE FACE OF THE EARTH SO SOME GREEDY OLD MEN CAN GET THEIR PECKERS HARD!
HOW CAN THAT NOT SCARE THE HELL OUTTA YOU?!
YOU KNOW WHAT SCARES ME, WOLVERINE?
TEN-YEAR-OLD GIRLS BEING TRADED FOR SEX. COUNTRIES STARVING BECAUSE OF RELIGIOUS WARS AND IMPERIALISM AND A FEW POWERFUL PEOPLE MAKING DECISIONS THAT AFFECT ENTIRE CONTINENTS!
YOUR HYPOCRICY IS MIND-BOGGLING. HOW MANY "HONOR" KILLINGS HAVE YOU COMMITTED? HOW MANY HAVE YOU MURDERED OUT OF PETTY REVENGE?
HOW MANY ANIMALS HAVE DIED AT YOUR HANDS TO SATIATE YOUR FERAL INSTINCTS--?!
I KILLED 'CAUSE I HAD TO! NEVER F'R MONEY OR LAND OR KICKS! AN' NEVER WITH THAT KINDA CRUELTY.
AND I WAS NEVER PROUD OF IT!
BUT YOU'RE SANCTIONING THE MASSACRE OF ENTIRE SPECIES OF CREATURES.
THEY'RE ANIMALS! THEY DON'T HAVE SOULS!
MOST PEOPLE THINK I'M NOTHING MORE THAN AN ANIMAL!

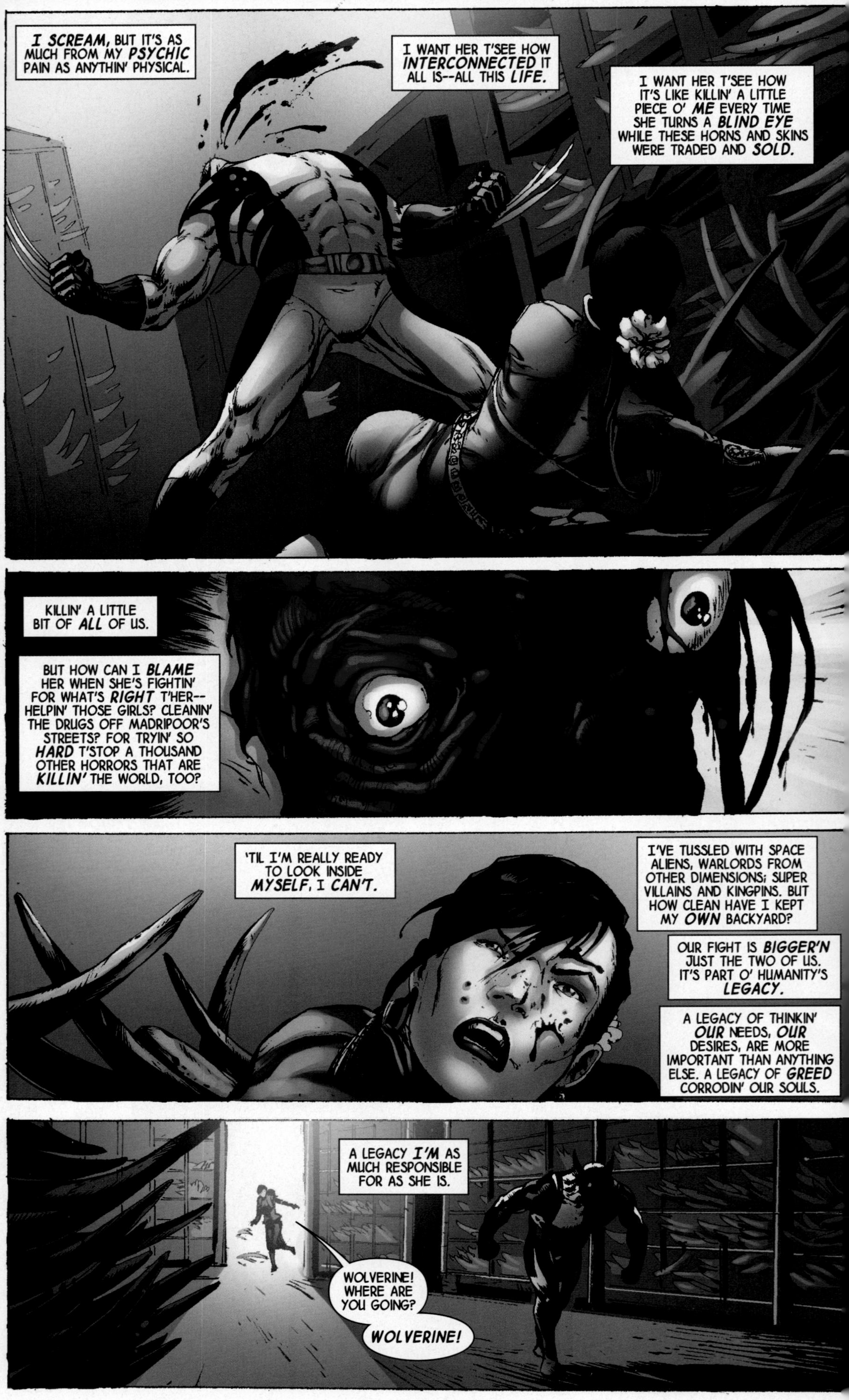

I SCREAM, BUT IT'S AS MUCH FROM MY PSYCHIC PAIN AS ANYTHIN' PHYSICAL.
I WANT HER T'SEE HOW INTERCONNECTED IT ALL IS--ALL THIS LIFE.
I WANT HER T'SEE HOW IT'S LIKE KILLIN' A LITTLE PIECE O' ME EVERY TIME SHE TURNS A BLIND EYE WHILE THESE HORNS AND SKINS WERE TRADED AND SOLD.
KILLIN' A LITTLE BIT OF ALL OF US.
BUT HOW CAN I BLAME HER WHEN SHE'S FIGHTIN' FOR WHAT'S RIGHT T'HER--HELPIN' THOSE GIRLS? CLEANIN' THE DRUGS OFF MADRIPOOR'S STREETS? FOR TRYIN' SO HARD T'STOP A THOUSAND OTHER HORRORS THAT ARE KILLIN' THE WORLD, TOO?
'TIL I'M REALLY READY TO LOOK INSIDE MYSELF, I CAN'T.
I'VE TUSSLED WITH SPACE ALIENS, WARLORDS FROM OTHER DIMENSIONS; SUPER VILLAINS AND KINGPINS. BUT HOW CLEAN HAVE I KEPT MY OWN BACKYARD?
OUR FIGHT IS BIGGER'N JUST THE TWO OF US. IT'S PART O' HUMANITY'S LEGACY.
A LEGACY OF THINKIN' OUR NEEDS, OUR DESIRES, ARE MORE IMPORTANT THAN ANYTHING ELSE. A LEGACY OF GREED CORRODIN' OUR SOULS.
A LEGACY I'M AS MUCH RESPONSIBLE FOR AS SHE IS.
WOLVERINE! WHERE ARE YOU GOING?
WOLVERINE!

WHAT DOES IT *MEAN* THAT WHAT I'M *BEST* AT ISN'T VERY *NICE?*

WHAT DOES IT MEAN FOR MY *SOUL?* FOR THE SOUL O' MY FRIENDS? FOR THE SOUL O' THE *WORLD?*

IT'S *EASY* FOR ME TO WALTZ IN HERE AND TELL HER SHE'S THE VILLAIN. TELL HER SHE'S *T'BLAME.*

IT'S A HELLUVA LOT LESS EASY TO TACKLE A *HISTORY* SO *BROKEN* BY FOLKS LIKE US THAT *LIFE* ITSELF MEANS SO LITTLE--

--AND SOMETIMES *MEANS NOTHIN'* AT ALL.

WHY DO THE TAG-LIGHTS KEEP *DISAPPEARING?* WHAT'S HAPPENING TO THE ELEPHANTS?

--ABOUT EVERY *FIFTEEN* MINUTES.

I TOLD YOU, KITTY. THIS IS AN *EXTINCTION-LEVEL PHENOMENON.*

ONE IS SLAUGHTERED--

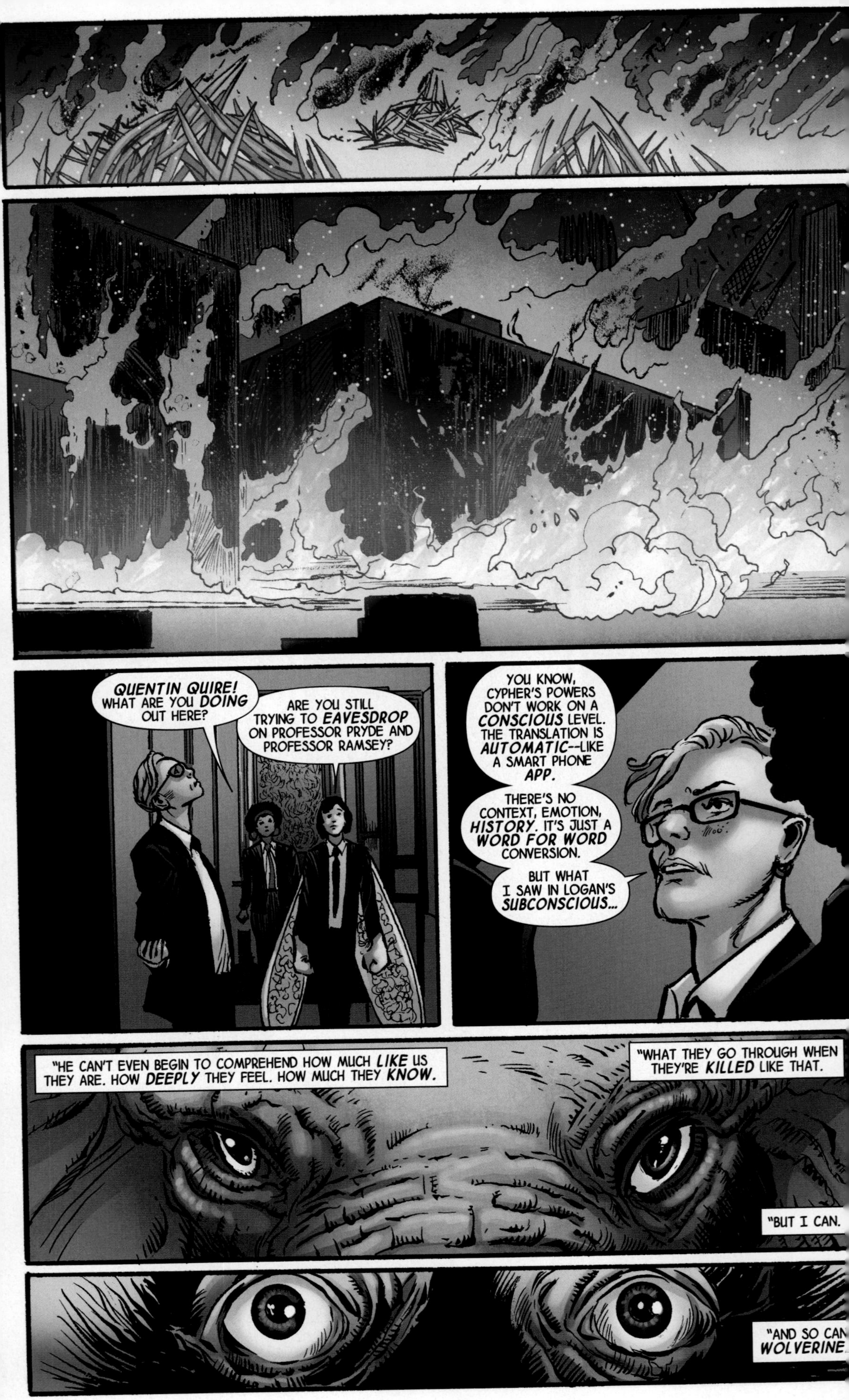
QUENTIN QUIRE! WHAT ARE YOU DOING OUT HERE?
ARE YOU STILL TRYING TO EAVESDROP ON PROFESSOR PRYDE AND PROFESSOR RAMSEY?
YOU KNOW, CYPHER'S POWERS DON'T WORK ON A CONSCIOUS LEVEL. THE TRANSLATION IS AUTOMATIC--LIKE A SMART PHONE APP.
THERE'S NO CONTEXT, EMOTION, HISTORY. IT'S JUST A WORD FOR WORD CONVERSION.
BUT WHAT I SAW IN LOGAN'S SUBCONSCIOUS...
"HE CAN'T EVEN BEGIN TO COMPREHEND HOW MUCH LIKE US THEY ARE. HOW DEEPLY THEY FEEL. HOW MUCH THEY KNOW.
"WHAT THEY GO THROUGH WHEN THEY'RE KILLED LIKE THAT.
"BUT I CAN.
"AND SO CAN WOLVERINE.

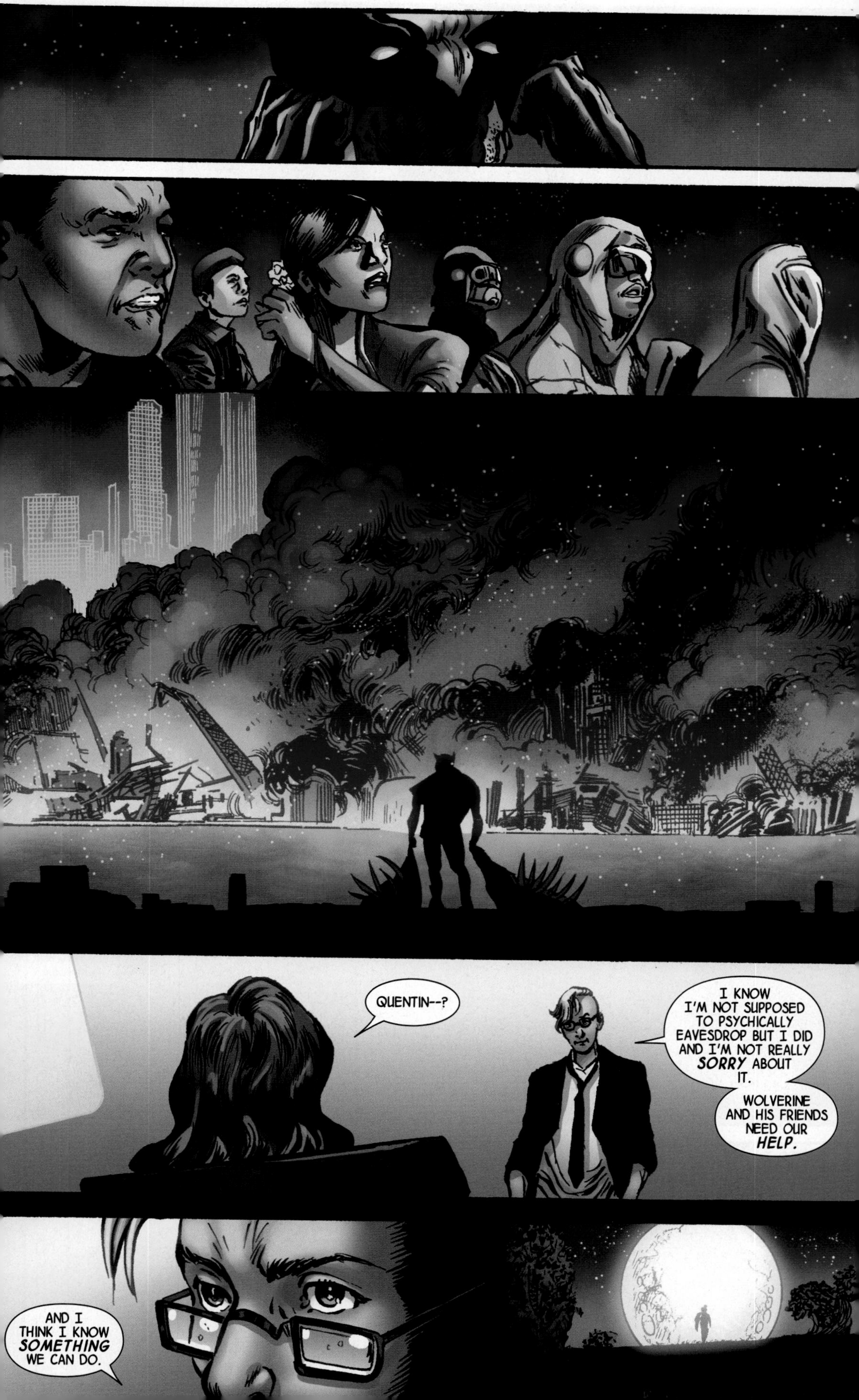
QUENTIN--?
I KNOW I'M NOT SUPPOSED TO PSYCHICALLY EAVESDROP BUT I DID AND I'M NOT REALLY SORRY ABOUT IT.
WOLVERINE AND HIS FRIENDS NEED OUR HELP.
AND I THINK I KNOW SOMETHING WE CAN DO.

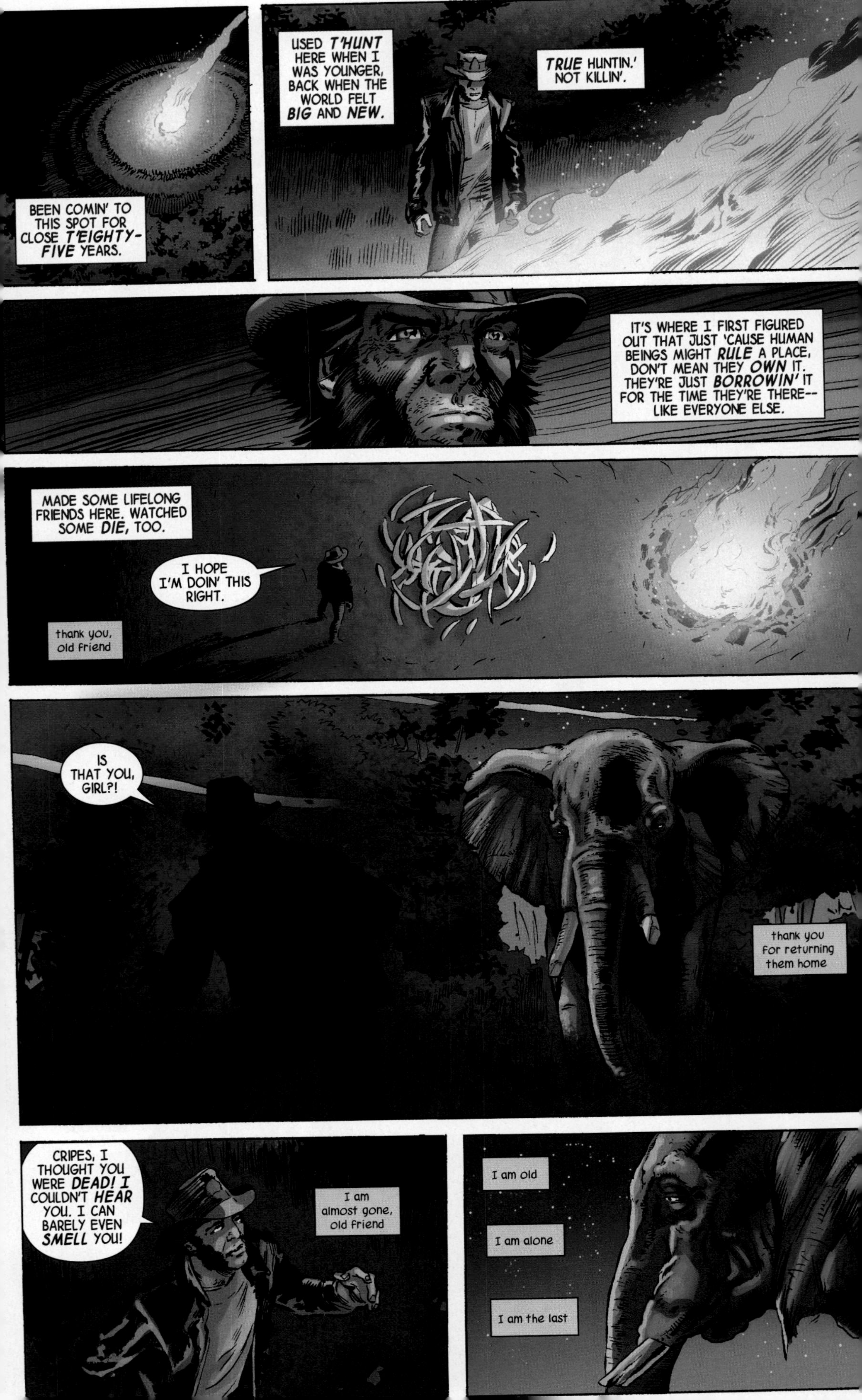
BEEN COMIN' TO THIS SPOT FOR CLOSE T'EIGHTY-FIVE YEARS.
USED T'HUNT HERE WHEN I WAS YOUNGER, BACK WHEN THE WORLD FELT BIG AND NEW.
TRUE HUNTIN.' NOT KILLIN'.
IT'S WHERE I FIRST FIGURED OUT THAT JUST 'CAUSE HUMAN BEINGS MIGHT RULE A PLACE, DON'T MEAN THEY OWN IT. THEY'RE JUST BORROWIN' IT FOR THE TIME THEY'RE THERE-- LIKE EVERYONE ELSE.
MADE SOME LIFELONG FRIENDS HERE. WATCHED SOME DIE, TOO.
I HOPE I'M DOIN' THIS RIGHT.
thank you, old friend
IS THAT YOU, GIRL?!
thank you for returning them home
CRIPES, I THOUGHT YOU WERE DEAD! I COULDN'T HEAR YOU. I CAN BARELY EVEN SMELL YOU!
I am almost gone, old friend
I am old
I am alone
I am the last

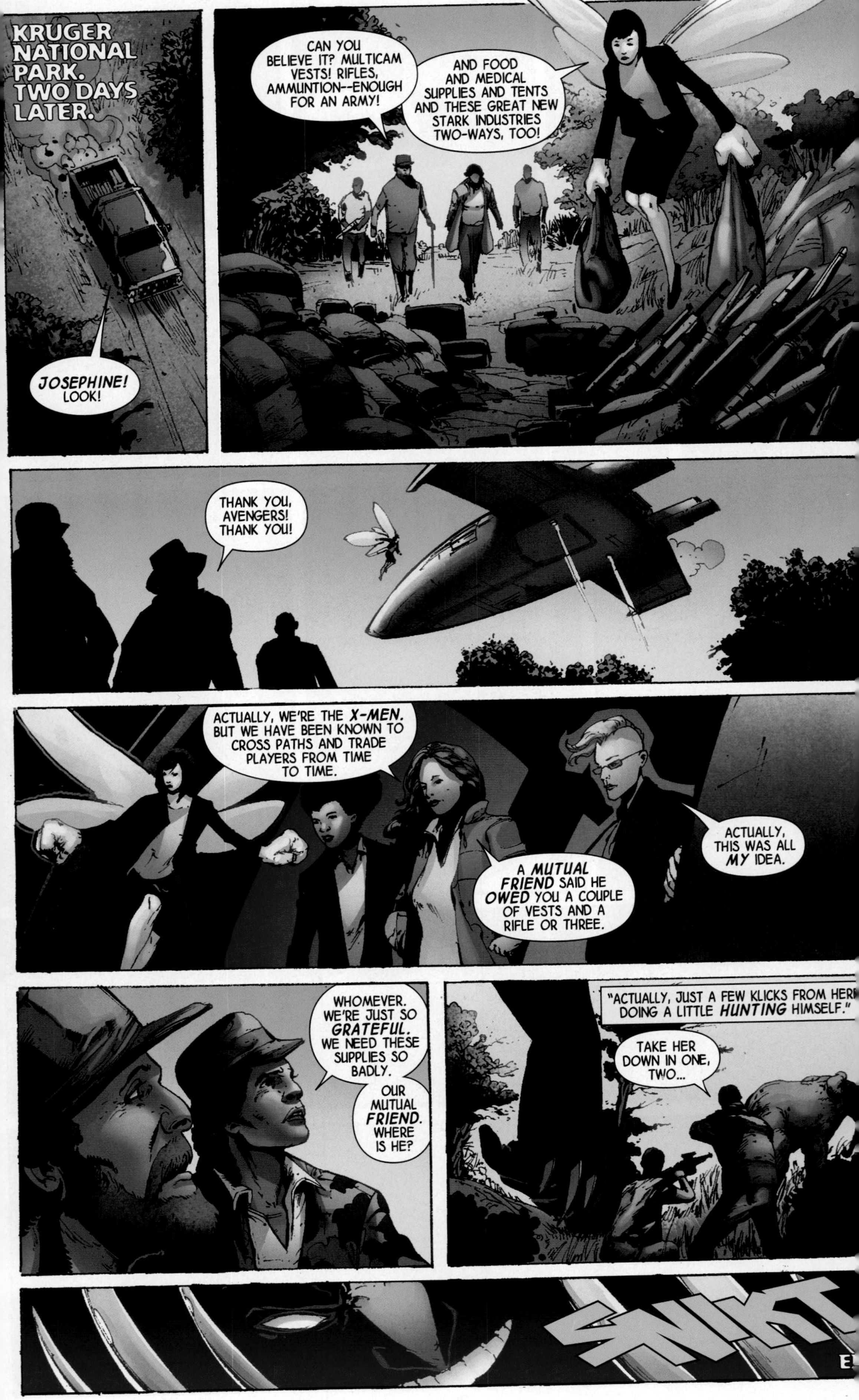
KRUGER NATIONAL PARK. TWO DAYS LATER.
JOSEPHINE! LOOK!
CAN YOU BELIEVE IT? MULTICAM VESTS! RIFLES, AMMUNTION--ENOUGH FOR AN ARMY!
AND FOOD AND MEDICAL SUPPLIES AND TENTS AND THESE GREAT NEW STARK INDUSTRIES TWO-WAYS, TOO!
THANK YOU, AVENGERS! THANK YOU!
ACTUALLY, WE'RE THE X-MEN. BUT WE HAVE BEEN KNOWN TO CROSS PATHS AND TRADE PLAYERS FROM TIME TO TIME.
A MUTUAL FRIEND SAID HE OWED YOU A COUPLE OF VESTS AND A RIFLE OR THREE.
ACTUALLY, THIS WAS ALL MY IDEA.
WHOMEVER. WE'RE JUST SO GRATEFUL. WE NEED THESE SUPPLIES SO BADLY.
OUR MUTUAL FRIEND. WHERE IS HE?
"ACTUALLY, JUST A FEW KLICKS FROM HER
DOING A LITTLE HUNTING HIMSELF."
TAKE HER DOWN IN ONE, TWO...
SNIKT

WRATH PART 1

14

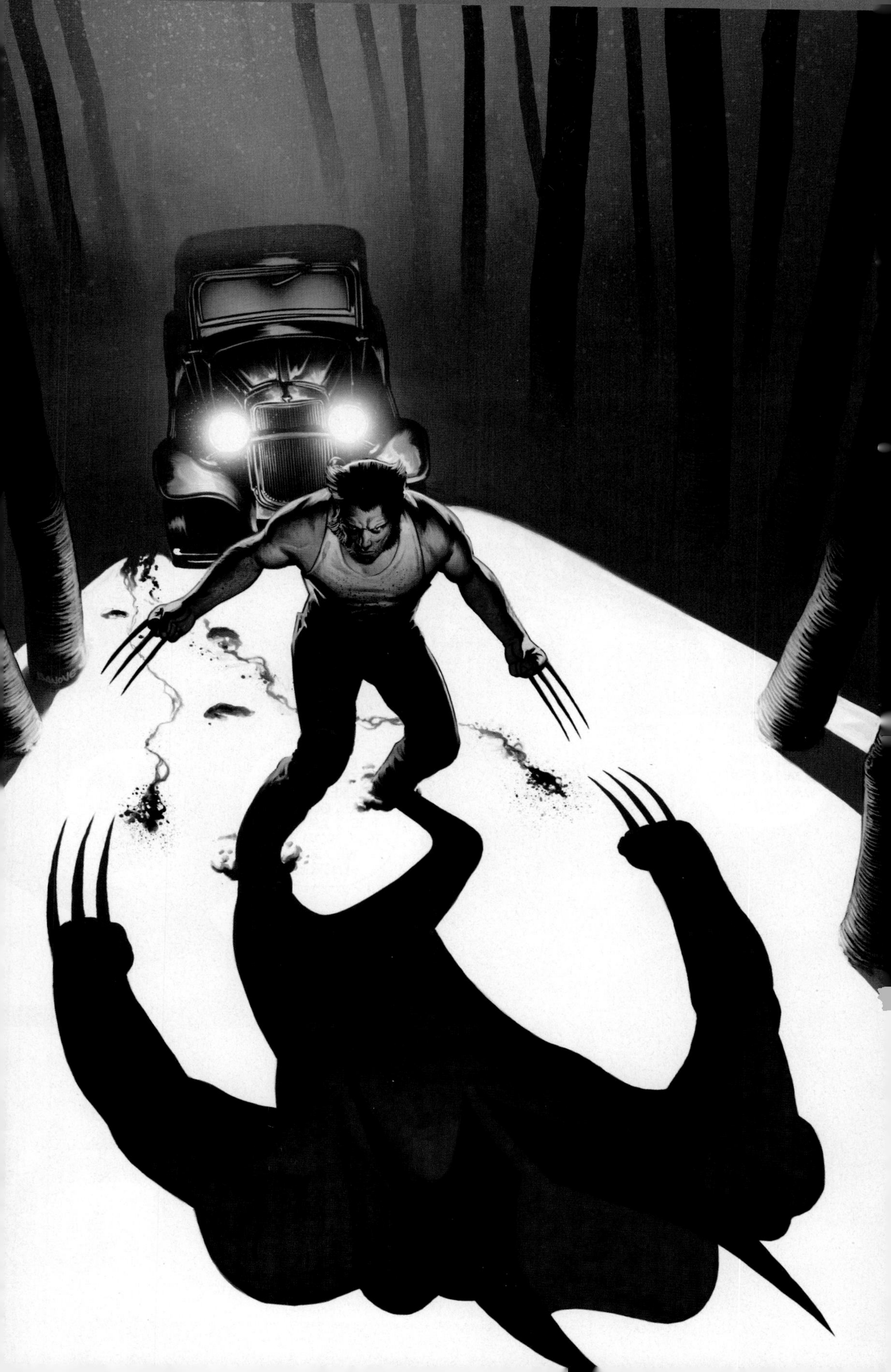

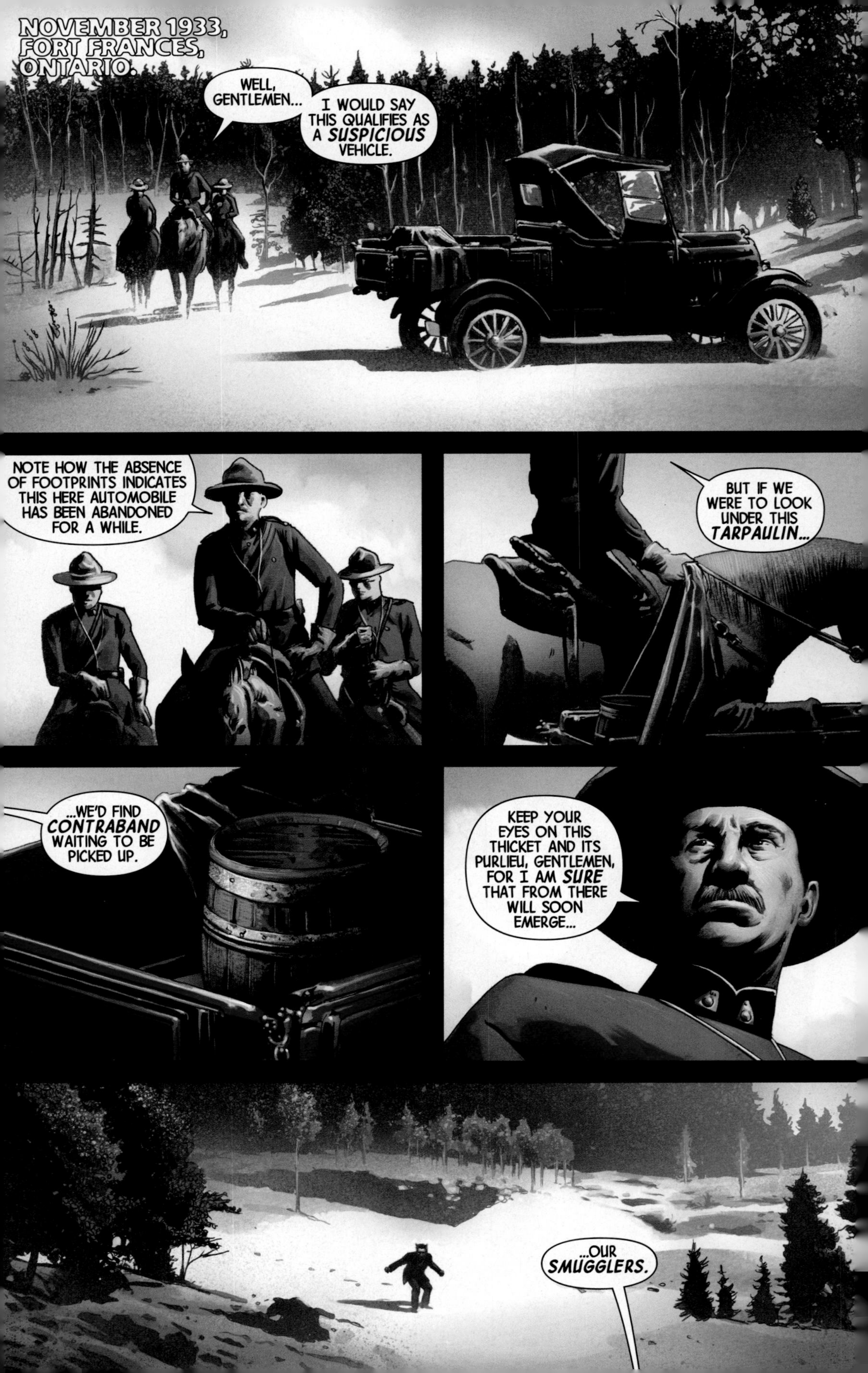
NOVEMBER 1933, FORT FRANCES, ONTARIO.
WELL, GENTLEMEN...
I WOULD SAY THIS QUALIFIES AS A SUSPICIOUS VEHICLE.
NOTE HOW THE ABSENCE OF FOOTPRINTS INDICATES THIS HERE AUTOMOBILE HAS BEEN ABANDONED FOR A WHILE.
BUT IF WE WERE TO LOOK UNDER THIS TARPAULIN...
...WE'D FIND CONTRABAND WAITING TO BE PICKED UP.
KEEP YOUR EYES ON THIS THICKET AND ITS PURLIEU, GENTLEMEN, FOR I AM SURE THAT FROM THERE WILL SOON EMERGE...
...OUR SMUGGLERS.

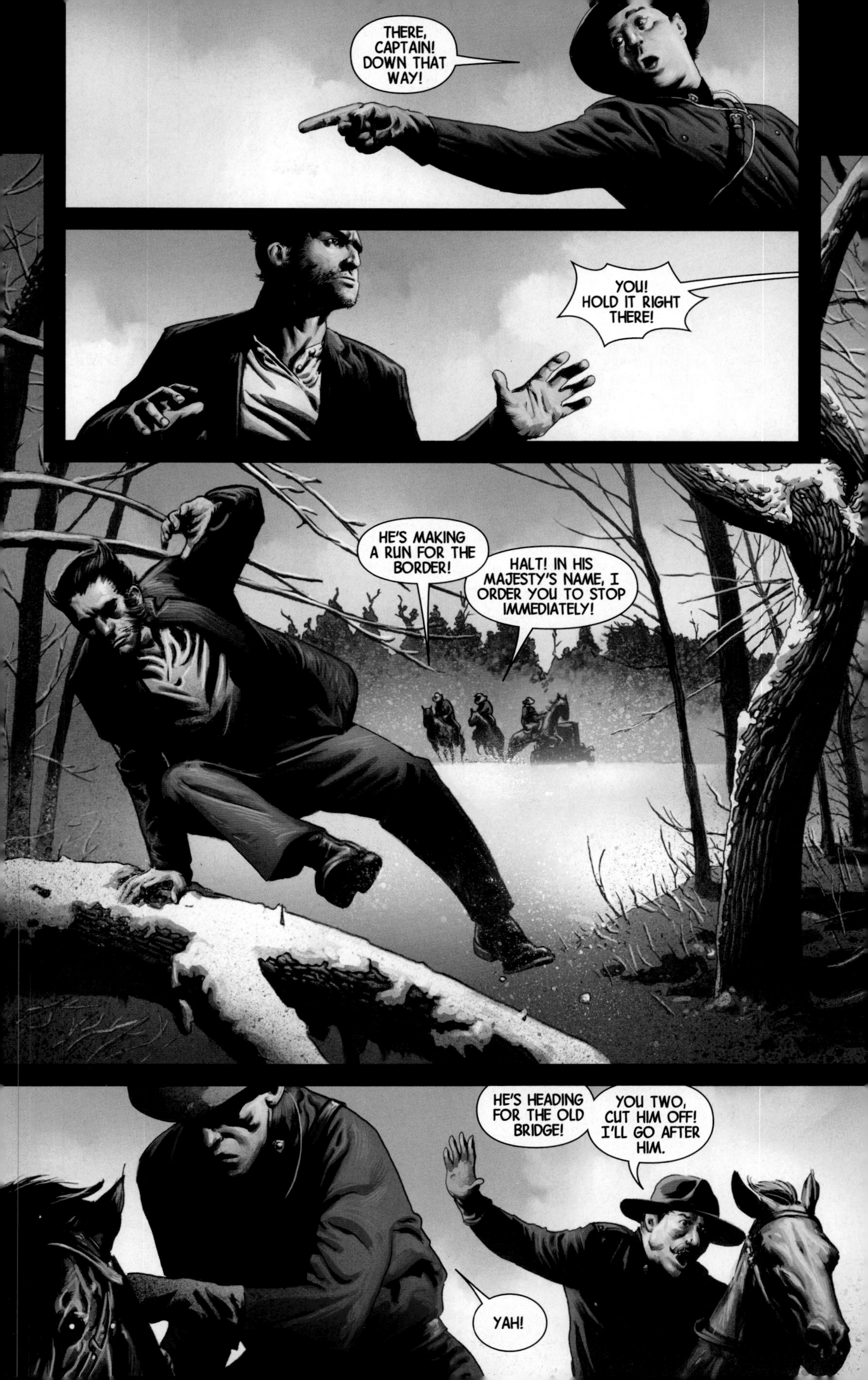
THERE, CAPTAIN! DOWN THAT WAY!
YOU! HOLD IT RIGHT THERE!
HE'S MAKING A RUN FOR THE BORDER!
HALT! IN HIS MAJESTY'S NAME, I ORDER YOU TO STOP IMMEDIATELY!
HE'S HEADING FOR THE OLD BRIDGE!
YOU TWO, CUT HIM OFF! I'LL GO AFTER HIM.
YAH!

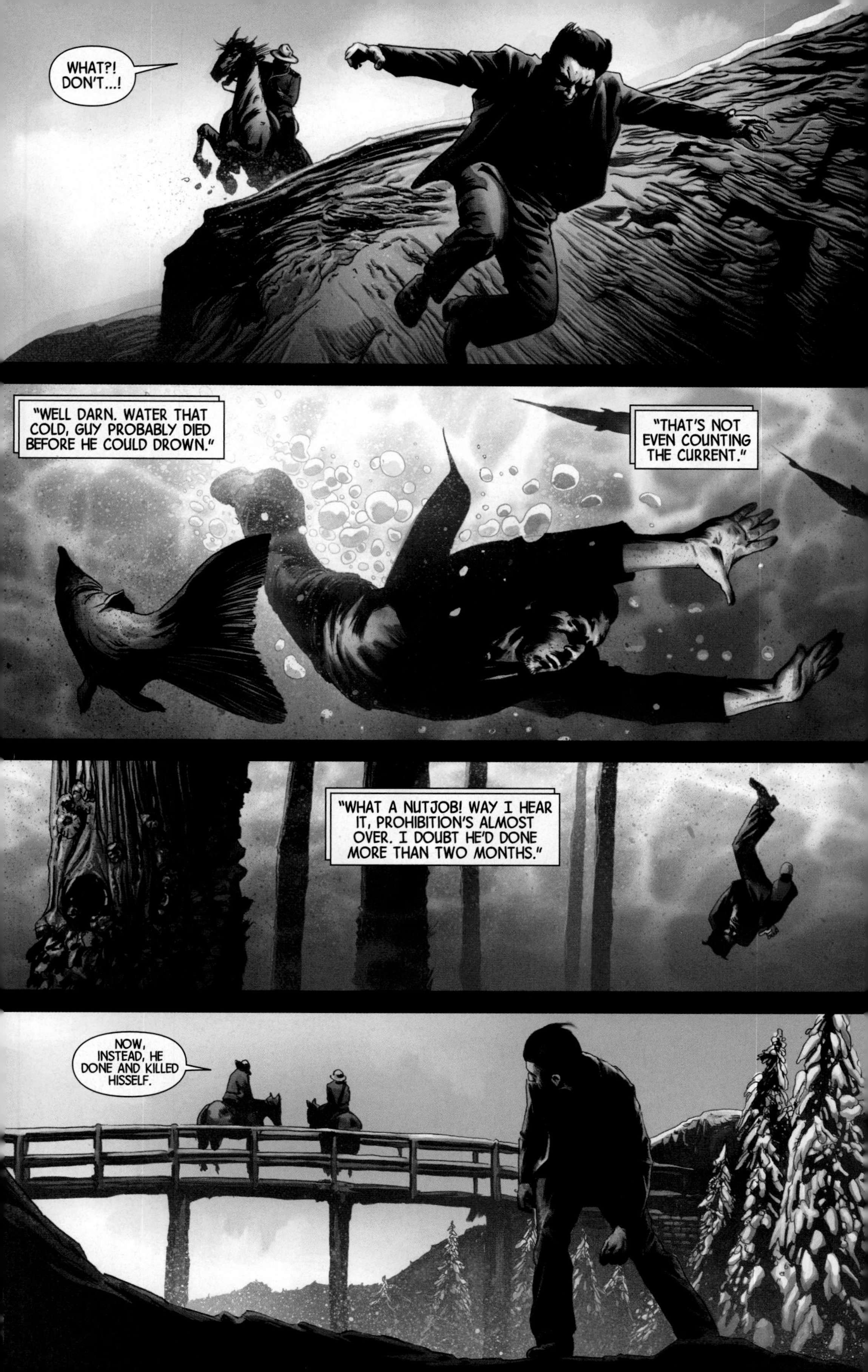
WHAT?! DON'T...!
"WELL DARN. WATER THAT COLD, GUY PROBABLY DIED BEFORE HE COULD DROWN."
"THAT'S NOT EVEN COUNTING THE CURRENT."
"WHAT A NUTJOB! WAY I HEAR IT, PROHIBITION'S ALMOST OVER. I DOUBT HE'D DONE MORE THAN TWO MONTHS."
NOW, INSTEAD, HE DONE AND KILLED HISSELF.

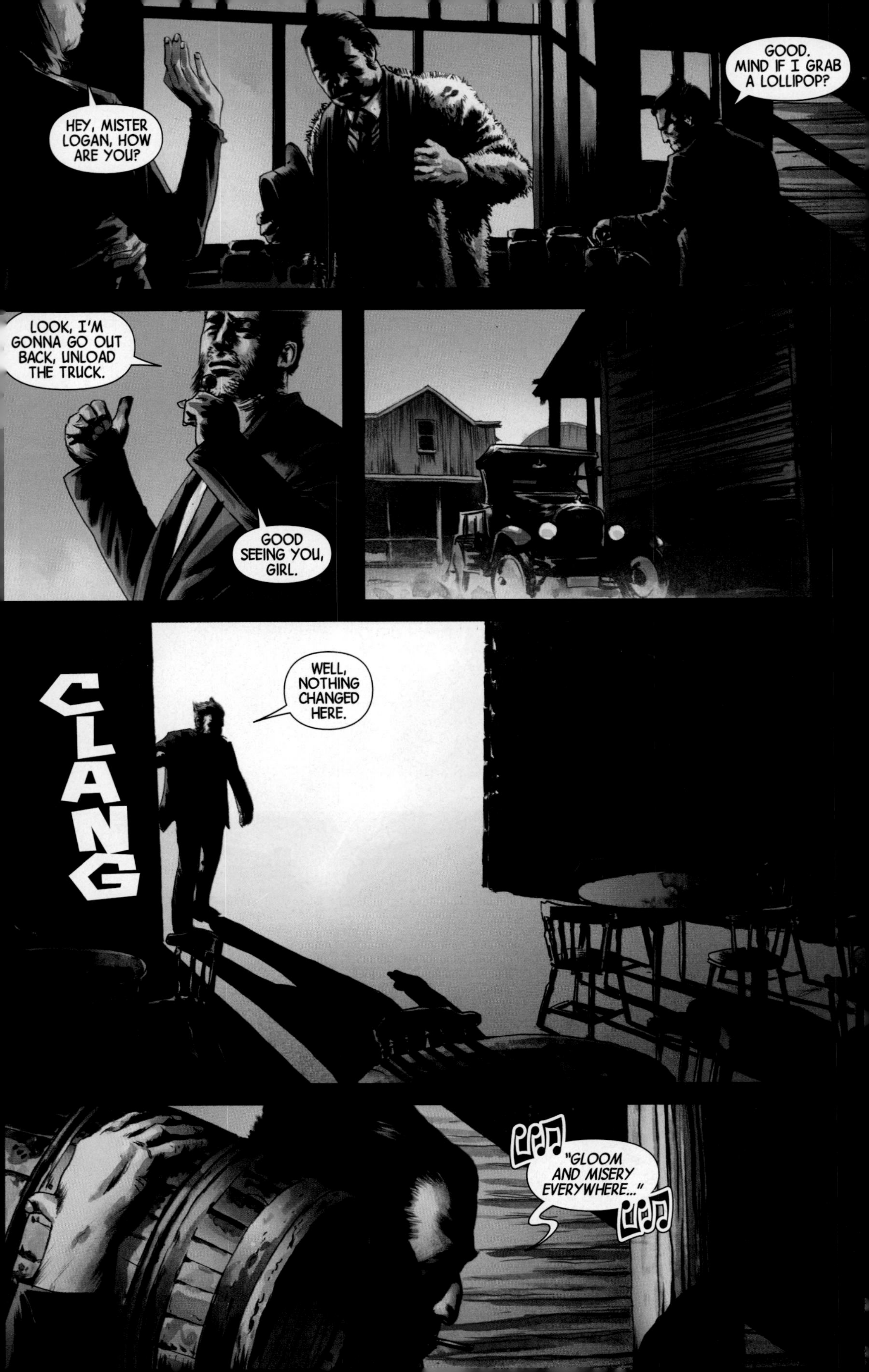
HEY, MISTER LOGAN, HOW ARE YOU?
GOOD. MIND IF I GRAB A LOLLIPOP?
LOOK, I'M GONNA GO OUT BACK, UNLOAD THE TRUCK.
GOOD SEEING YOU, GIRL.
CLANG
WELL, NOTHING CHANGED HERE.
"GLOOM AND MISERY EVERYWHERE..."

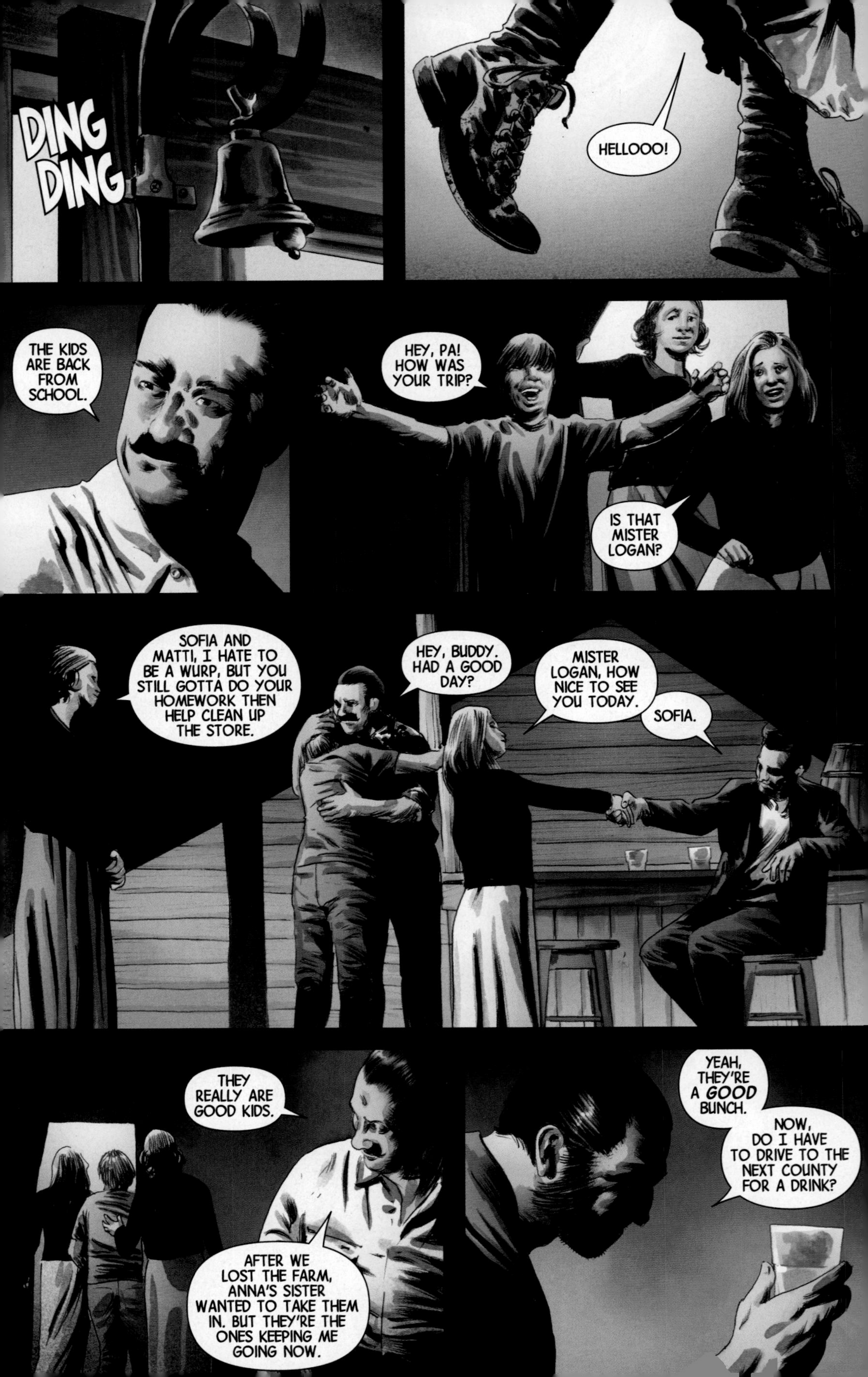
DING DING
HELLOOO!
THE KIDS ARE BACK FROM SCHOOL.
HEY, PA! HOW WAS YOUR TRIP?
IS THAT MISTER LOGAN?
SOFIA AND MATTI, I HATE TO BE A WURP, BUT YOU STILL GOTTA DO YOUR HOMEWORK THEN HELP CLEAN UP THE STORE.
HEY, BUDDY. HAD A GOOD DAY?
MISTER LOGAN, HOW NICE TO SEE YOU TODAY.
SOFIA.
THEY REALLY ARE GOOD KIDS.
AFTER WE LOST THE FARM, ANNA'S SISTER WANTED TO TAKE THEM IN. BUT THEY'RE THE ONES KEEPING ME GOING NOW.
YEAH, THEY'RE A GOOD BUNCH.
NOW, DO I HAVE TO DRIVE TO THE NEXT COUNTY FOR A DRINK?

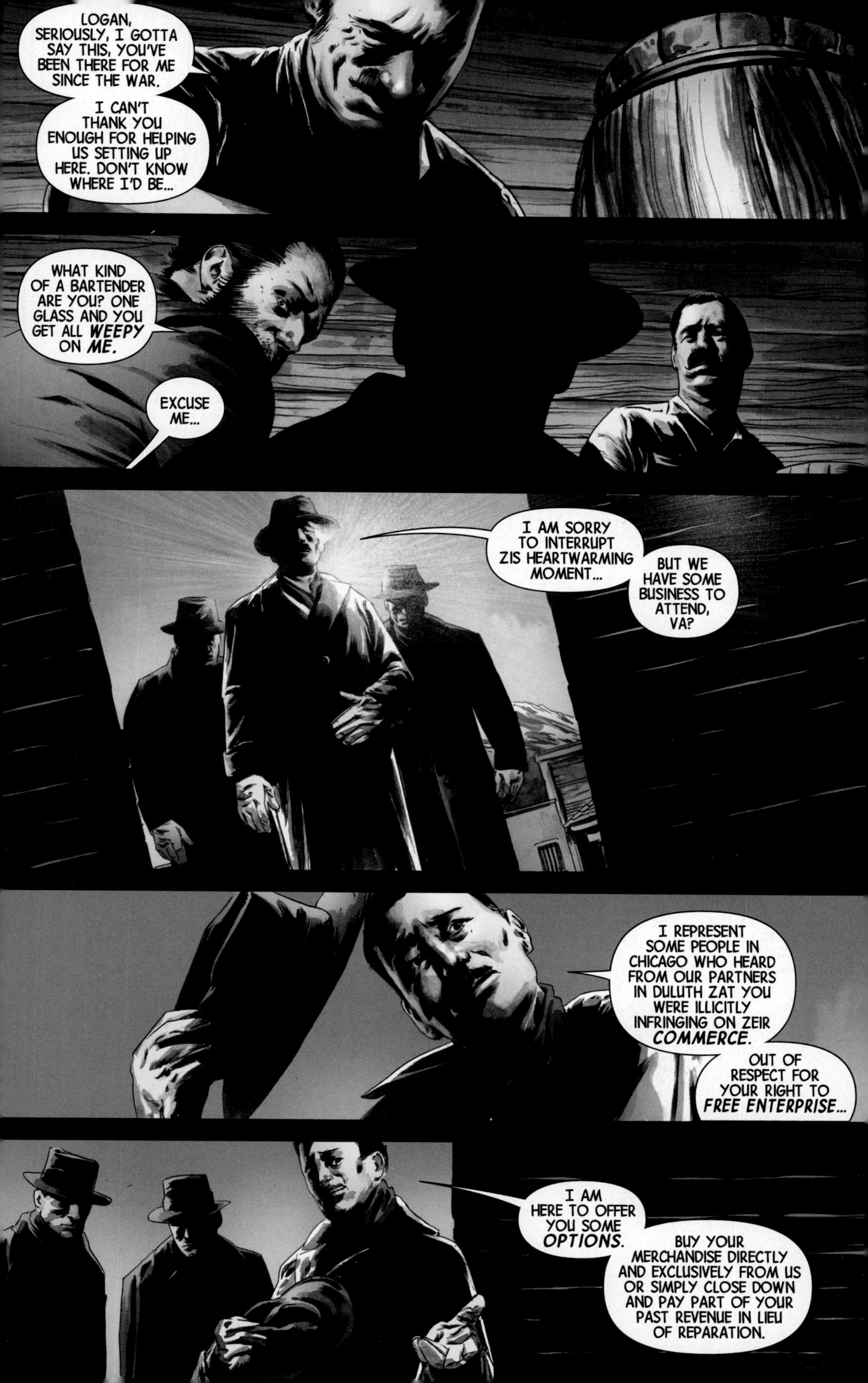
LOGAN, SERIOUSLY, I GOTTA SAY THIS, YOU'VE BEEN THERE FOR ME SINCE THE WAR.
I CAN'T THANK YOU ENOUGH FOR HELPING US SETTING UP HERE. DON'T KNOW WHERE I'D BE...
WHAT KIND OF A BARTENDER ARE YOU? ONE GLASS AND YOU GET ALL *WEEPY* ON *ME.*
EXCUSE ME...
I AM SORRY TO INTERRUPT ZIS HEARTWARMING MOMENT...
BUT WE HAVE SOME BUSINESS TO ATTEND, VA?
I REPRESENT SOME PEOPLE IN CHICAGO WHO HEARD FROM OUR PARTNERS IN DULUTH ZAT YOU WERE ILLICITLY INFRINGING ON ZEIR *COMMERCE.*
OUT OF RESPECT FOR YOUR RIGHT TO *FREE ENTERPRISE...*
I AM HERE TO OFFER YOU SOME *OPTIONS.*
BUY YOUR MERCHANDISE DIRECTLY AND EXCLUSIVELY FROM US OR SIMPLY CLOSE DOWN AND PAY PART OF YOUR PAST REVENUE IN LIEU OF REPARATION.

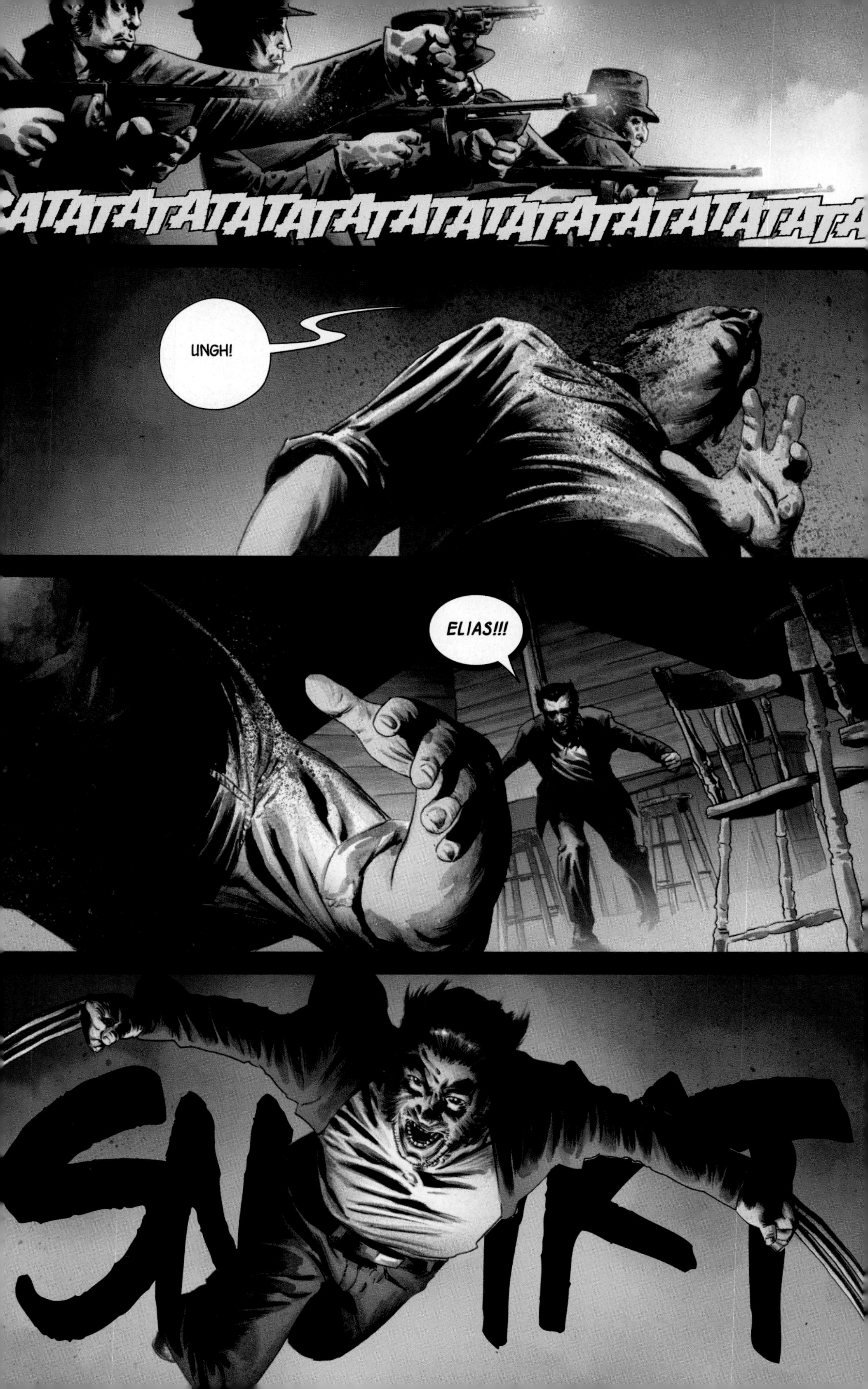
UNGH!
ELIAS!!!
SNIKT

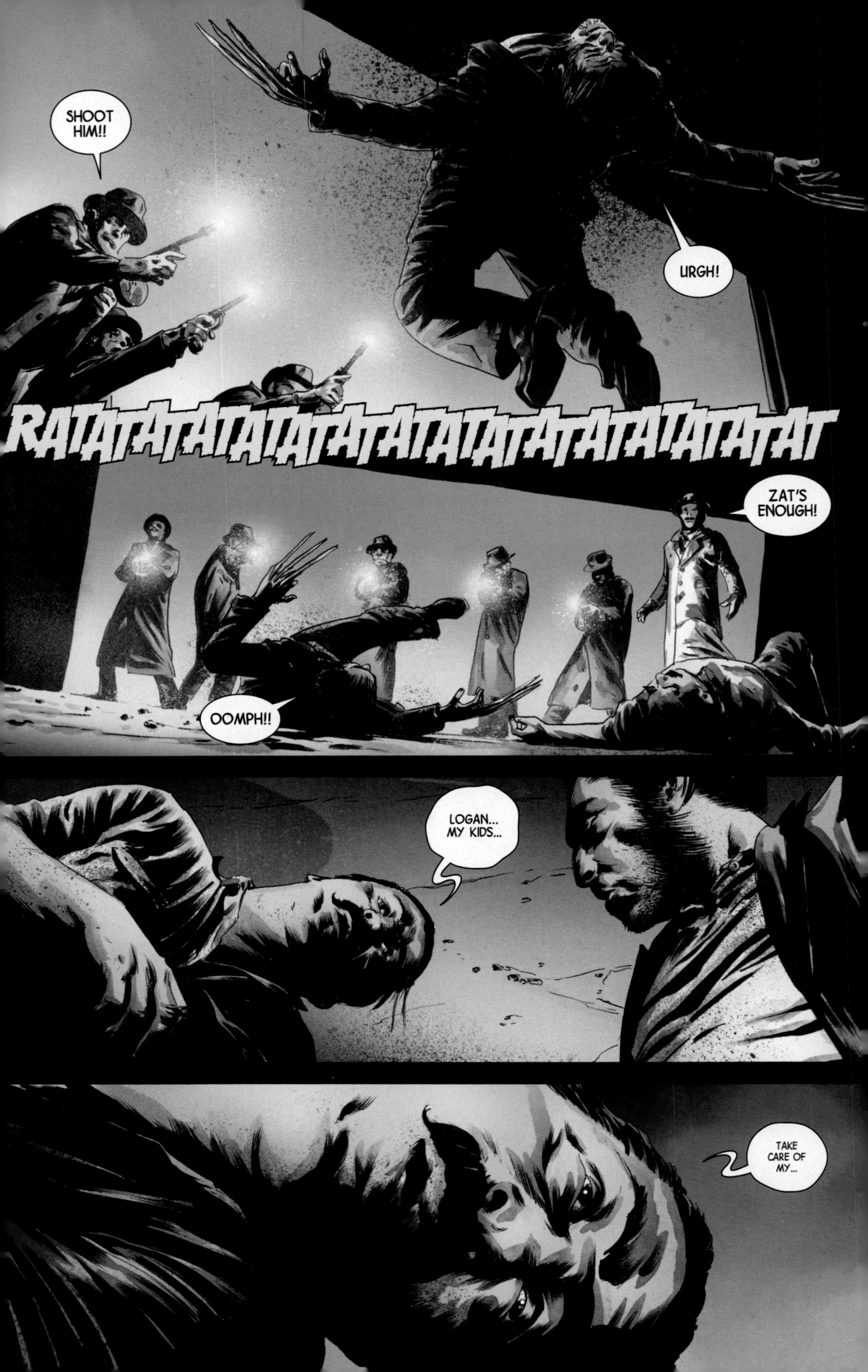
SHOOT HIM!!
URGH!
RATATATATATATATATATATATATATATATATATAT
ZAT'S ENOUGH!
OOMPH!!
LOGAN... MY KIDS...
TAKE CARE OF MY...

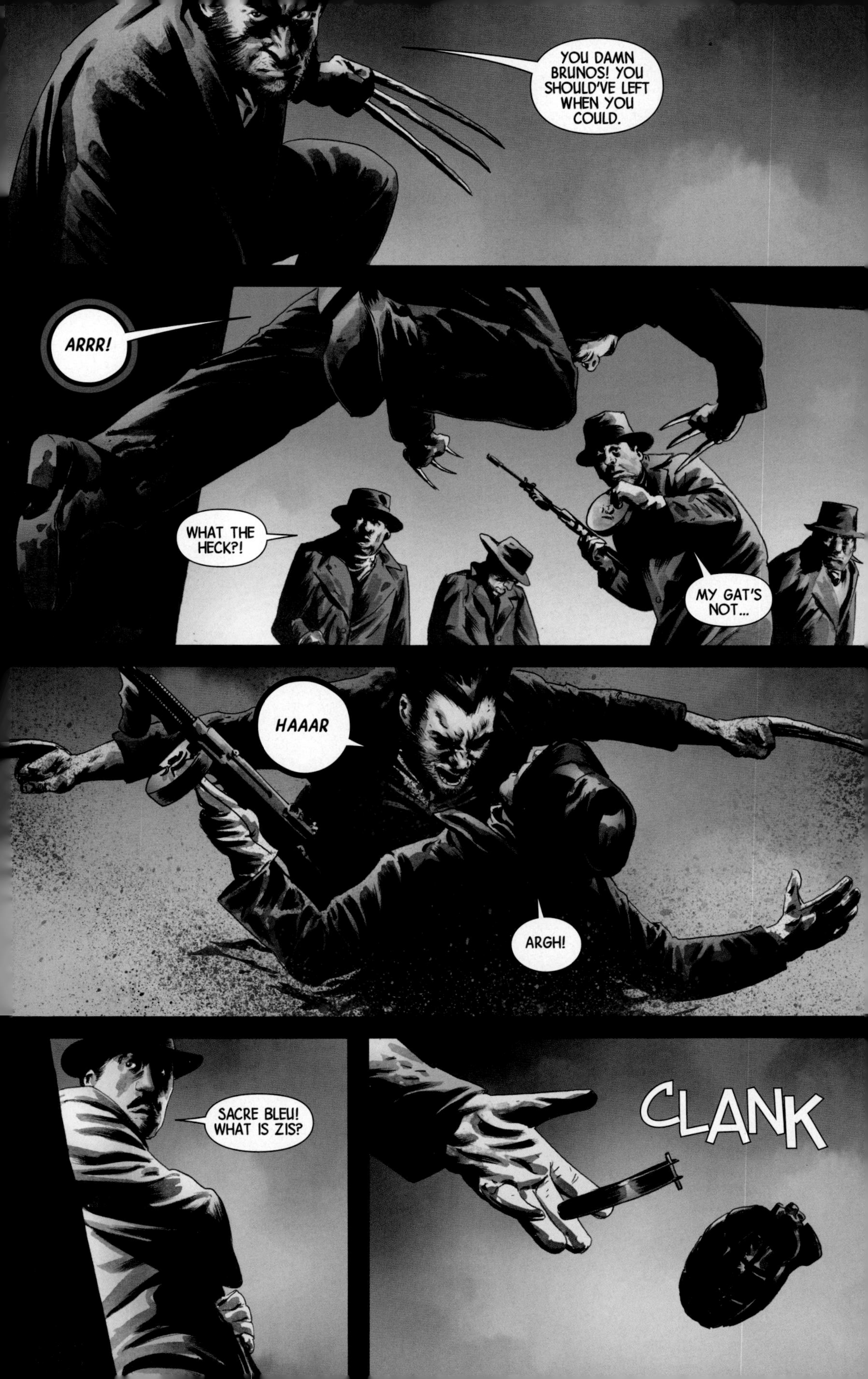
YOU DAMN BRUNOS! YOU SHOULD'VE LEFT WHEN YOU COULD.
ARRR!
WHAT THE HECK?!
MY GAT'S NOT...
HAAAR
ARGH!
SACRE BLEU! WHAT IS ZIS?
CLANK

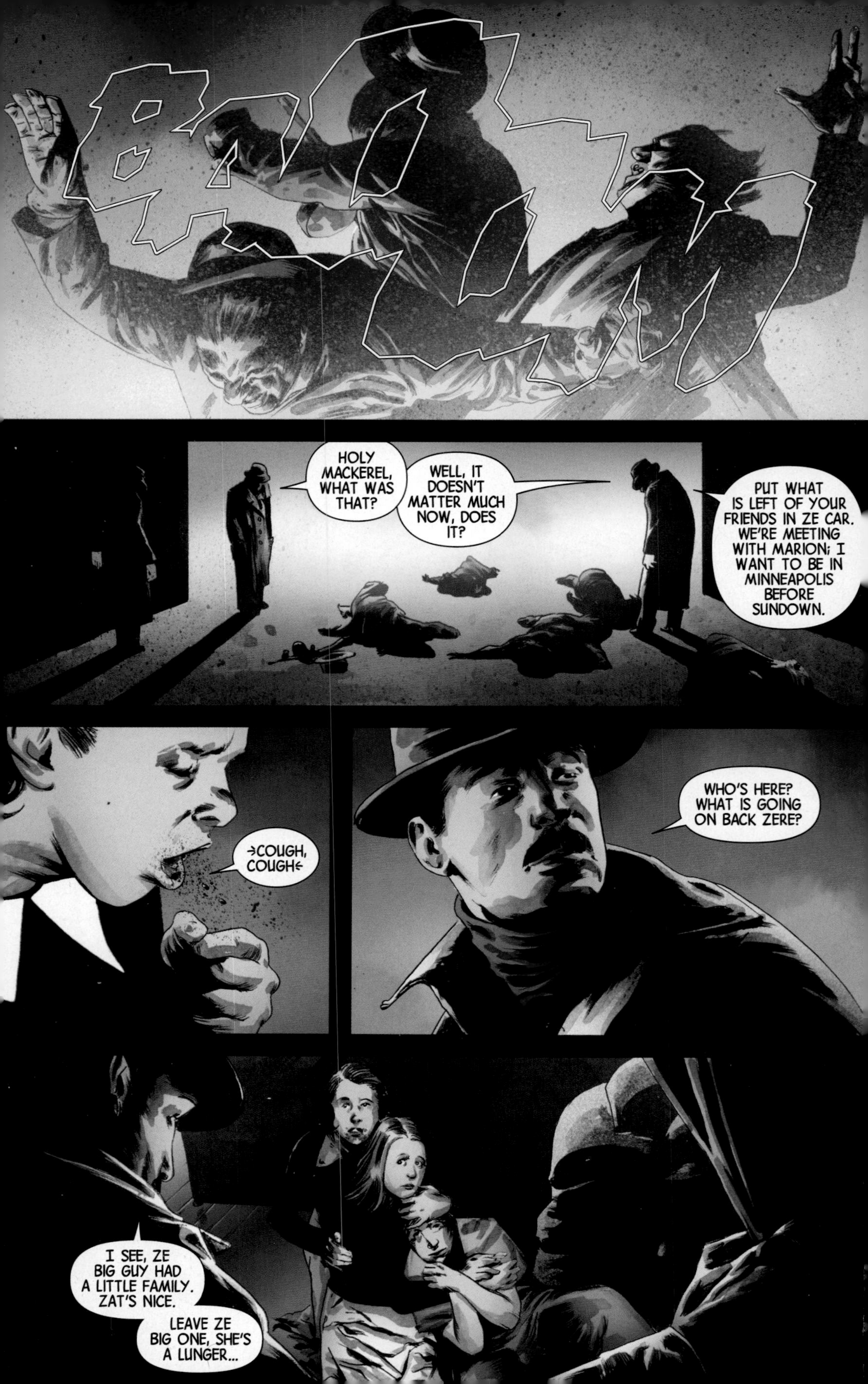
BLAM
HOLY MACKEREL, WHAT WAS THAT?
WELL, IT DOESN'T MATTER MUCH NOW, DOES IT?
PUT WHAT IS LEFT OF YOUR FRIENDS IN ZE CAR. WE'RE MEETING WITH MARION; I WANT TO BE IN MINNEAPOLIS BEFORE SUNDOWN.
>COUGH, COUGH<
WHO'S HERE? WHAT IS GOING ON BACK ZERE?
I SEE, ZE BIG GUY HAD A LITTLE FAMILY. ZAT'S NICE.
LEAVE ZE BIG ONE, SHE'S A LUNGER...

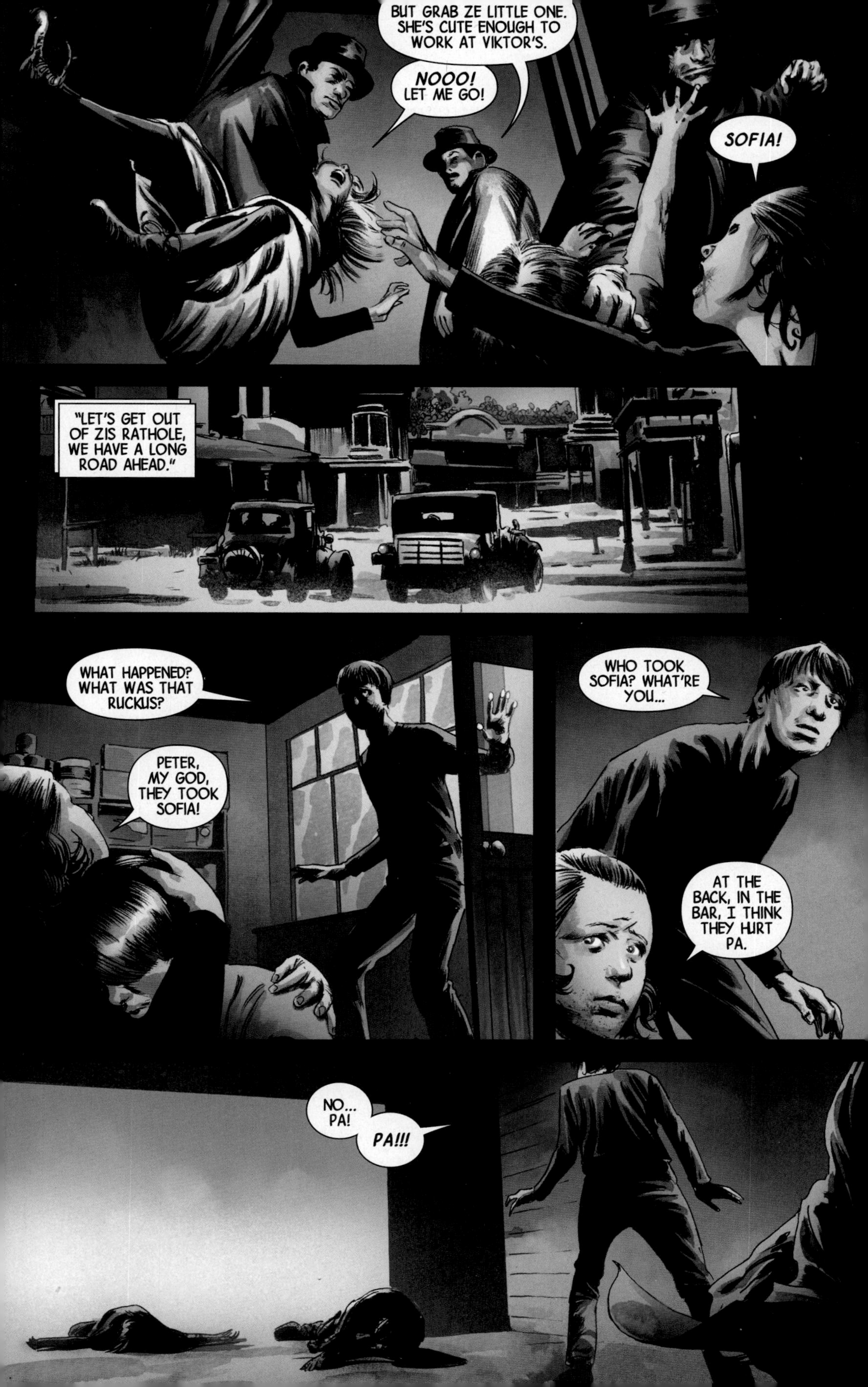
BUT GRAB ZE LITTLE ONE. SHE'S CUTE ENOUGH TO WORK AT VIKTOR'S.
NOOO! LET ME GO!
SOFIA!
"LET'S GET OUT OF ZIS RATHOLE, WE HAVE A LONG ROAD AHEAD."
WHAT HAPPENED? WHAT WAS THAT RUCKUS?
PETER, MY GOD, THEY TOOK SOFIA!
WHO TOOK SOFIA? WHAT'RE YOU...
AT THE BACK, IN THE BAR, I THINK THEY HURT PA.
NO... PA!
PA!!!

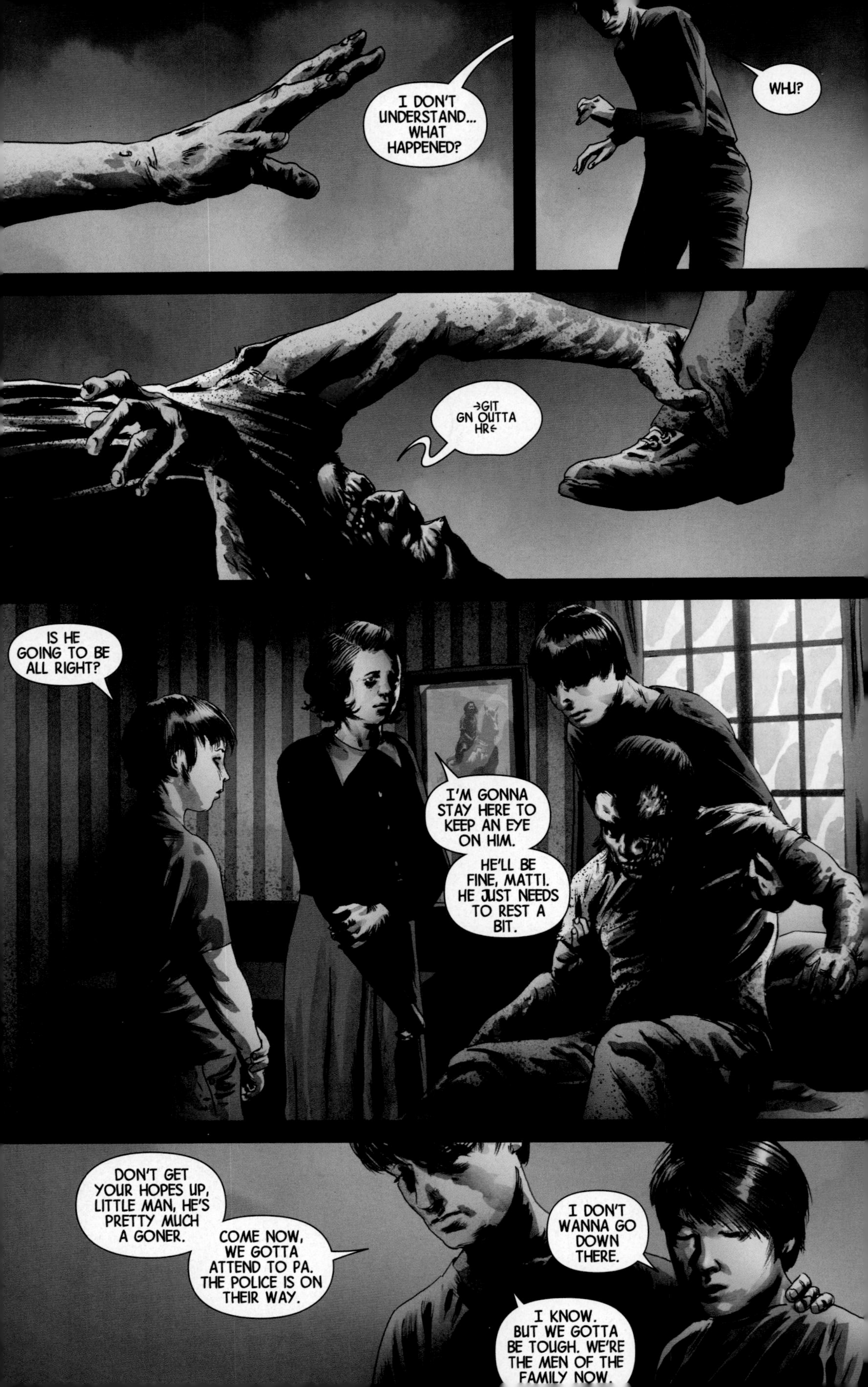
I DON'T UNDERSTAND... WHAT HAPPENED?
WHU?
→GIT GN OUTTA HR←
IS HE GOING TO BE ALL RIGHT?
I'M GONNA STAY HERE TO KEEP AN EYE ON HIM.
HE'LL BE FINE, MATTI. HE JUST NEEDS TO REST A BIT.
DON'T GET YOUR HOPES UP, LITTLE MAN, HE'S PRETTY MUCH A GONER.
COME NOW, WE GOTTA ATTEND TO PA. THE POLICE IS ON THEIR WAY.
I DON'T WANNA GO DOWN THERE.
I KNOW. BUT WE GOTTA BE TOUGH. WE'RE THE MEN OF THE FAMILY NOW.

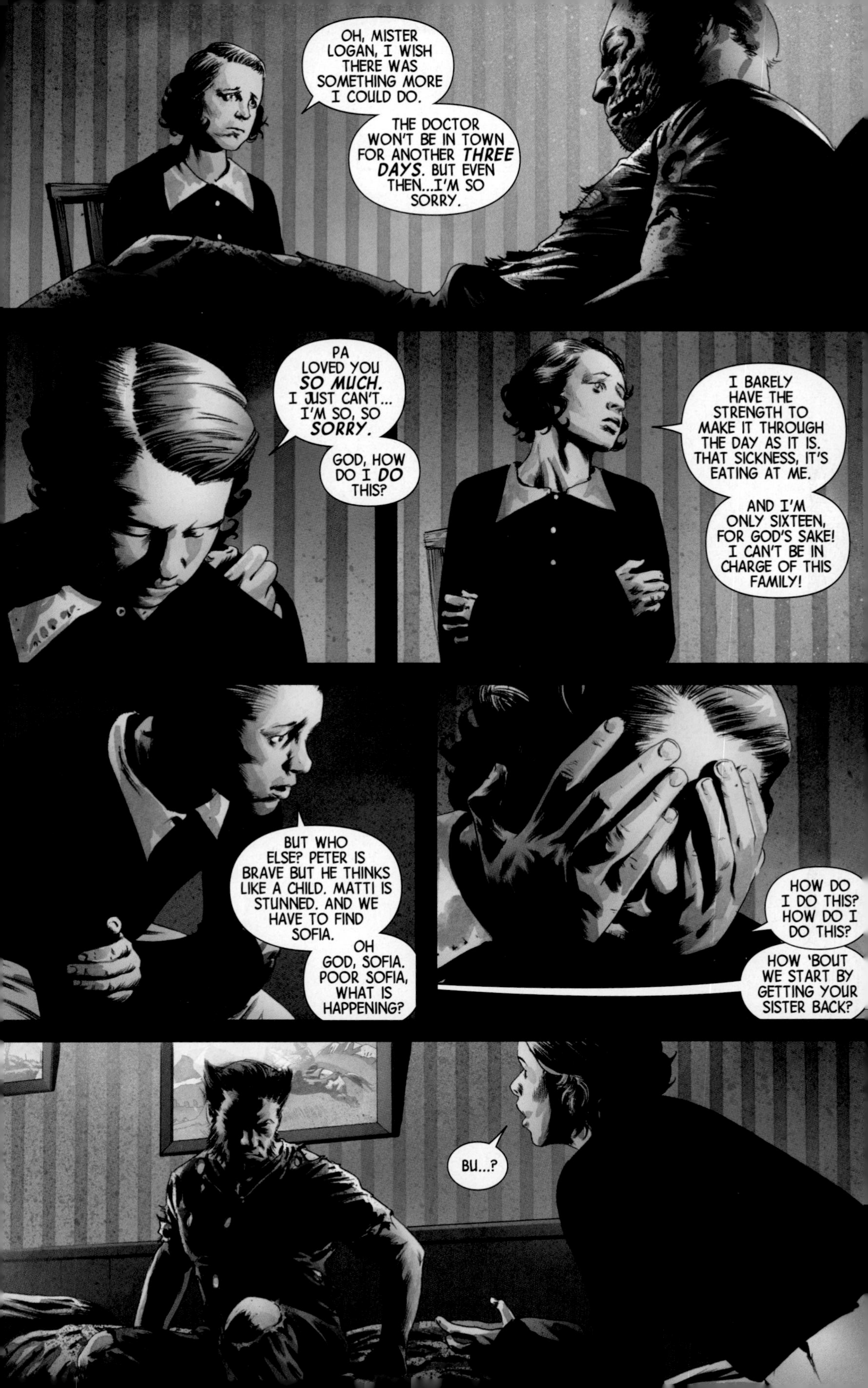
OH, MISTER LOGAN, I WISH THERE WAS SOMETHING MORE I COULD DO.
THE DOCTOR WON'T BE IN TOWN FOR ANOTHER THREE DAYS. BUT EVEN THEN...I'M SO SORRY.
PA LOVED YOU SO MUCH. I JUST CAN'T... I'M SO, SO SORRY.
GOD, HOW DO I DO THIS?
I BARELY HAVE THE STRENGTH TO MAKE IT THROUGH THE DAY AS IT IS. THAT SICKNESS, IT'S EATING AT ME.
AND I'M ONLY SIXTEEN, FOR GOD'S SAKE! I CAN'T BE IN CHARGE OF THIS FAMILY!
BUT WHO ELSE? PETER IS BRAVE BUT HE THINKS LIKE A CHILD. MATTI IS STUNNED. AND WE HAVE TO FIND SOFIA.
OH GOD, SOFIA. POOR SOFIA, WHAT IS HAPPENING?
HOW DO I DO THIS? HOW DO I DO THIS?
HOW 'BOUT WE START BY GETTING YOUR SISTER BACK?
BU...?

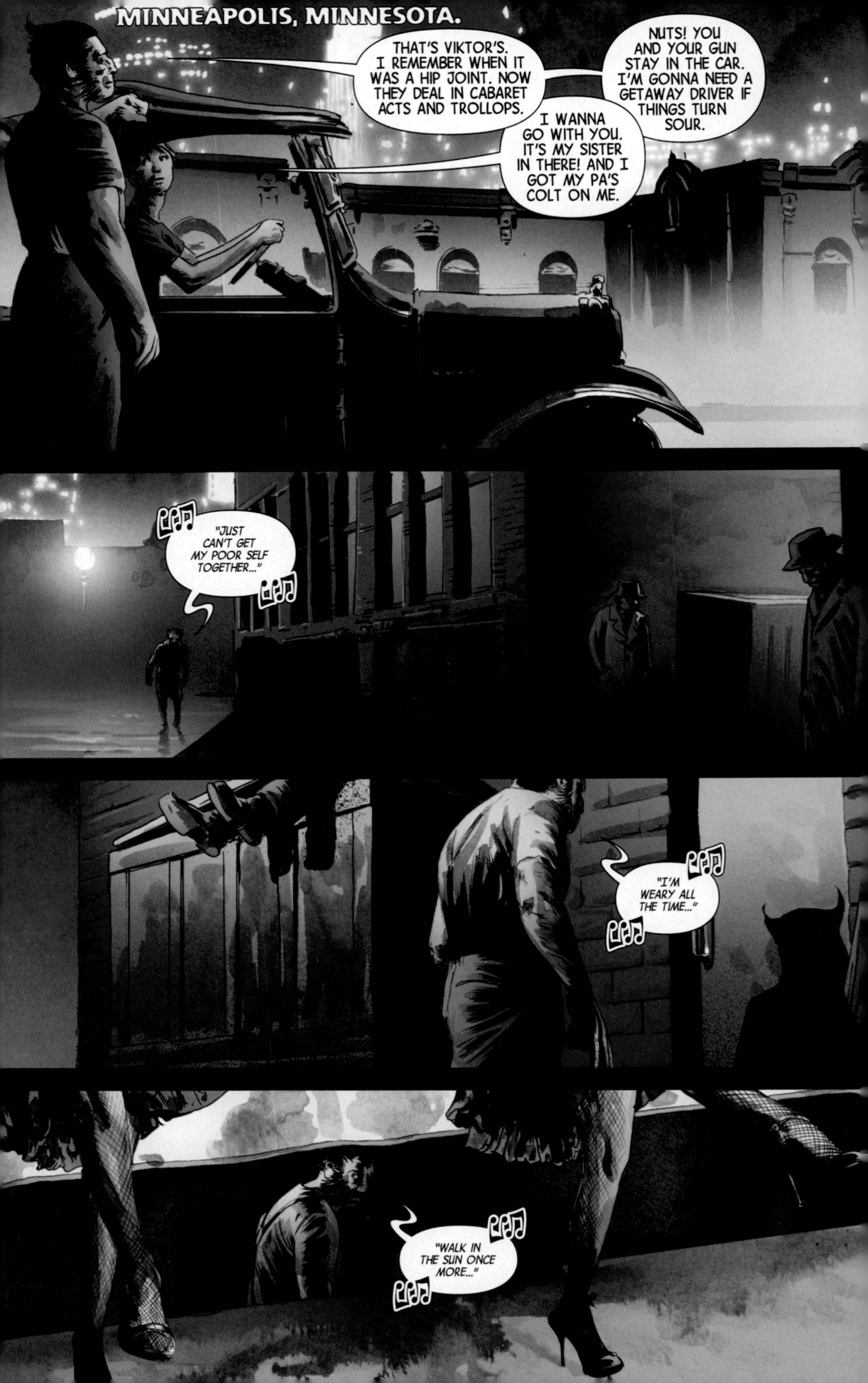
MINNEAPOLIS, MINNESOTA.
THAT'S VIKTOR'S. I REMEMBER WHEN IT WAS A HIP JOINT. NOW THEY DEAL IN CABARET ACTS AND TROLLOPS.
I WANNA GO WITH YOU. IT'S MY SISTER IN THERE! AND I GOT MY PA'S COLT ON ME.
NUTS! YOU AND YOUR GUN STAY IN THE CAR. I'M GONNA NEED A GETAWAY DRIVER IF THINGS TURN SOUR.
"JUST CAN'T GET MY POOR SELF TOGETHER..."
"I'M WEARY ALL THE TIME..."
"WALK IN THE SUN ONCE MORE..."

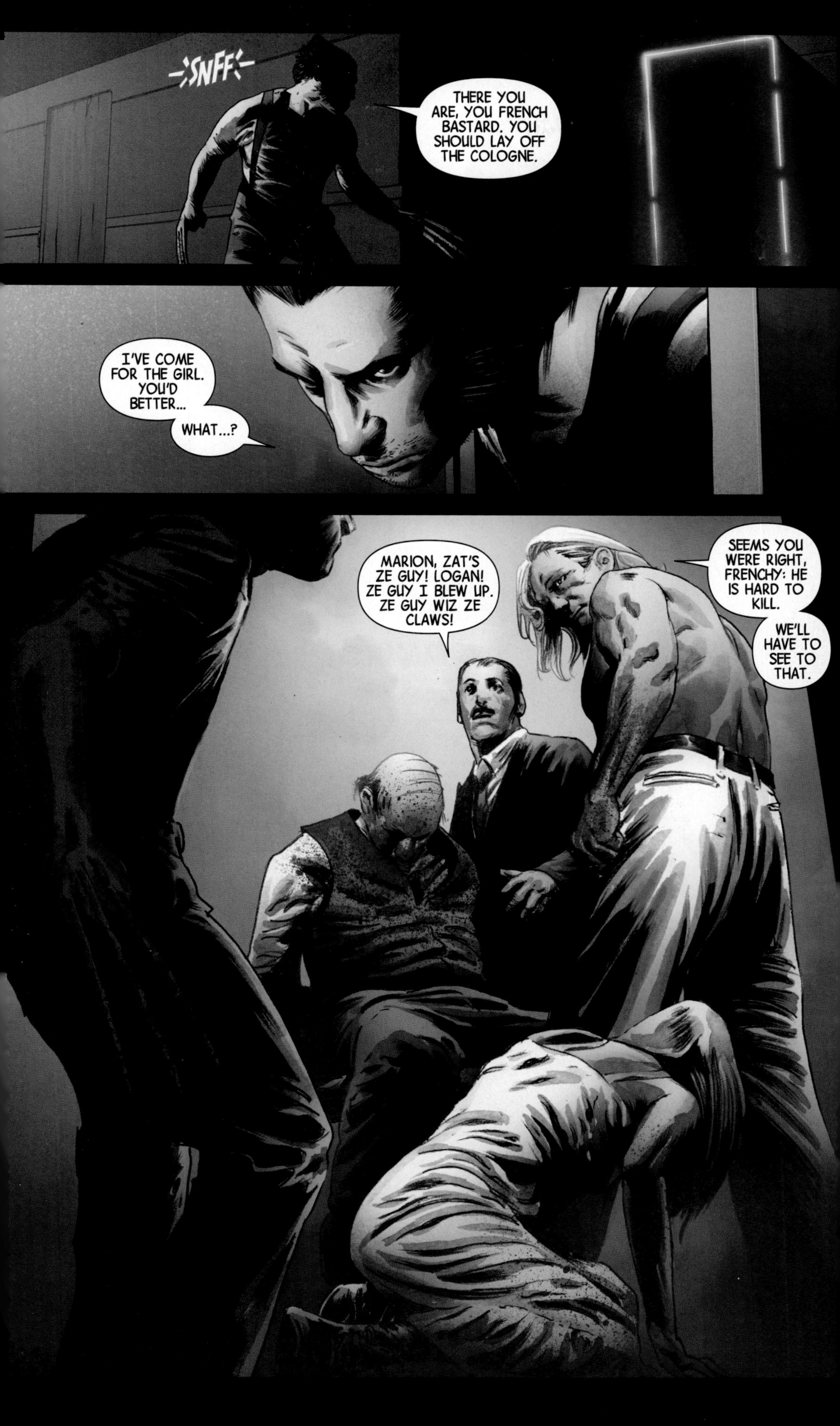
SNFF
THERE YOU ARE, YOU FRENCH BASTARD. YOU SHOULD LAY OFF THE COLOGNE.
I'VE COME FOR THE GIRL. YOU'D BETTER...
WHAT...?
MARION, ZAT'S ZE GUY! LOGAN! ZE GUY I BLEW UP. ZE GUY WIZ ZE CLAWS!
SEEMS YOU WERE RIGHT, FRENCHY: HE IS HARD TO KILL.
WE'LL HAVE TO SEE TO THAT.

15 WRATH PART

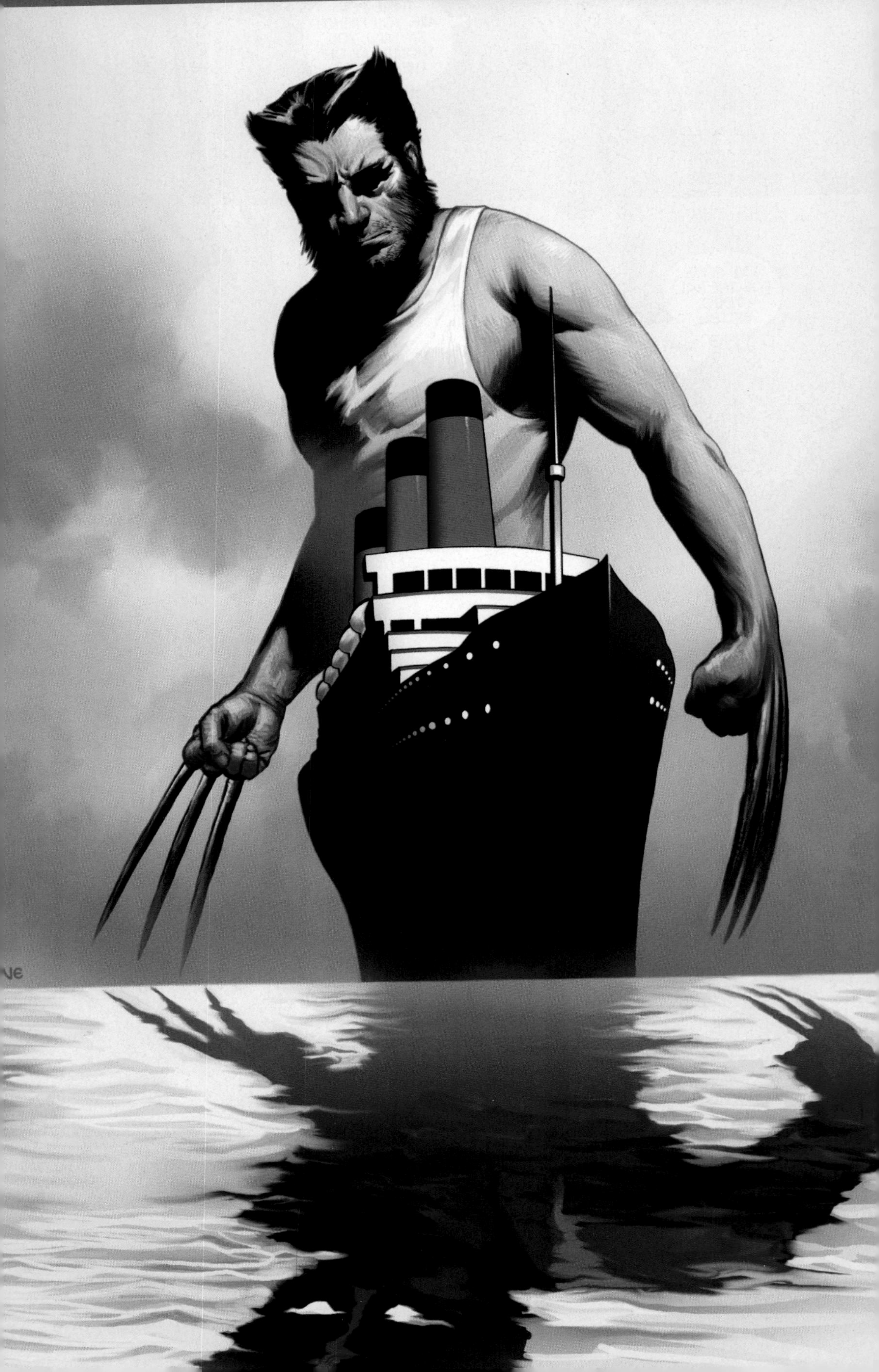

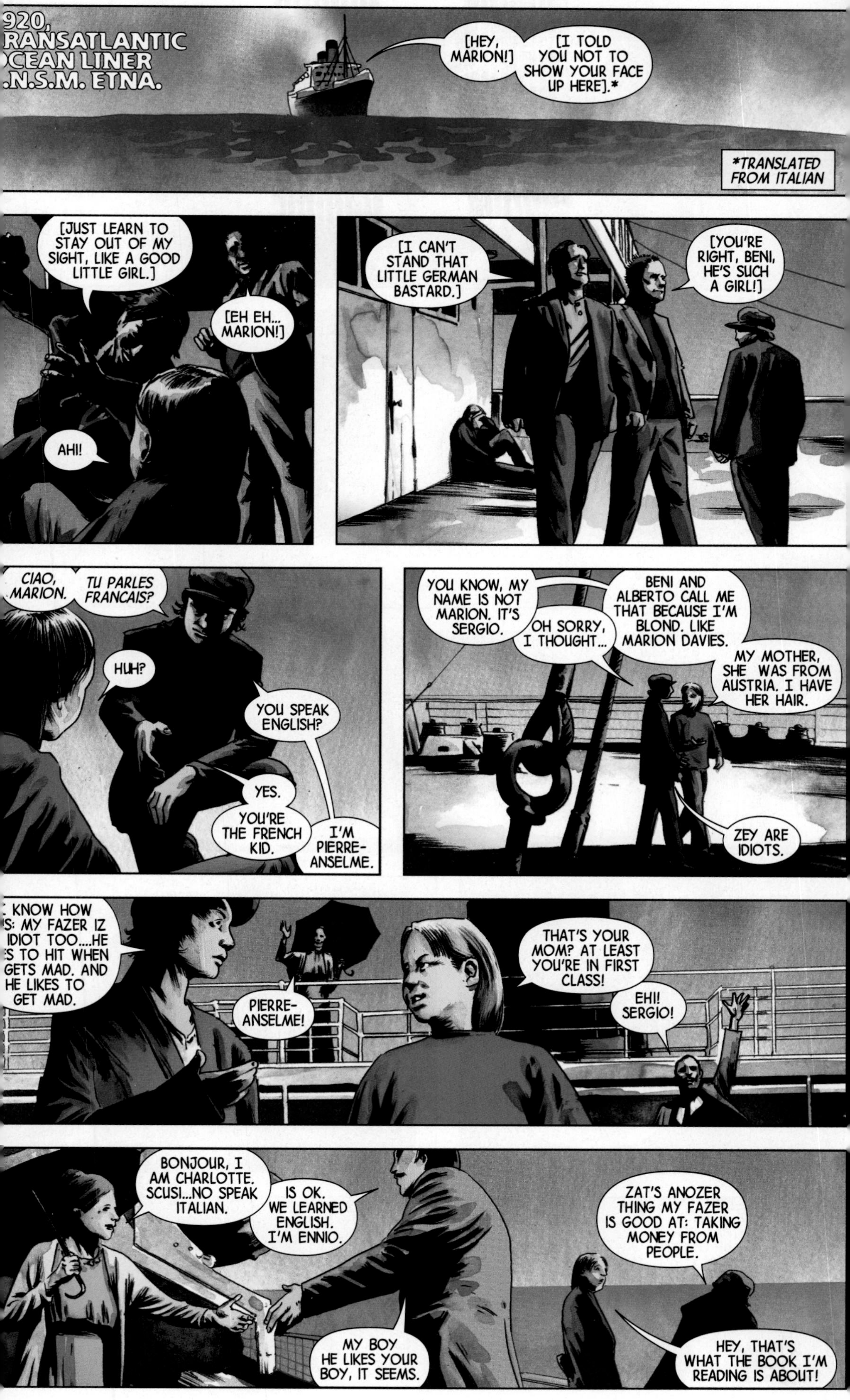
920,
RANSATLANTIC
CEAN LINER
.N.S.M. ETNA.
[HEY, MARION!]
[I TOLD YOU NOT TO SHOW YOUR FACE UP HERE].*
*TRANSLATED FROM ITALIAN
[JUST LEARN TO STAY OUT OF MY SIGHT, LIKE A GOOD LITTLE GIRL.]
[EH EH... MARION!]
AHI!
[I CAN'T STAND THAT LITTLE GERMAN BASTARD.]
[YOU'RE RIGHT, BENI, HE'S SUCH A GIRL!]
CIAO, MARION.
TU PARLES FRANCAIS?
HUH?
YOU SPEAK ENGLISH?
YES.
YOU'RE THE FRENCH KID.
I'M PIERRE-ANSELME.
YOU KNOW, MY NAME IS NOT MARION. IT'S SERGIO.
BENI AND ALBERTO CALL ME THAT BECAUSE I'M BLOND. LIKE MARION DAVIES.
OH SORRY, I THOUGHT...
MY MOTHER, SHE WAS FROM AUSTRIA. I HAVE HER HAIR.
ZEY ARE IDIOTS.
KNOW HOW S: MY FAZER IZ IDIOT TOO....HE S TO HIT WHEN GETS MAD. AND HE LIKES TO GET MAD.
PIERRE-ANSELME!
THAT'S YOUR MOM? AT LEAST YOU'RE IN FIRST CLASS!
EHI! SERGIO!
BONJOUR, I AM CHARLOTTE. SCUSI...NO SPEAK ITALIAN.
IS OK. WE LEARNED ENGLISH. I'M ENNIO.
MY BOY HE LIKES YOUR BOY, IT SEEMS.
ZAT'S ANOZER THING MY FAZER IS GOOD AT: TAKING MONEY FROM PEOPLE.
HEY, THAT'S WHAT THE BOOK I'M READING IS ABOUT!

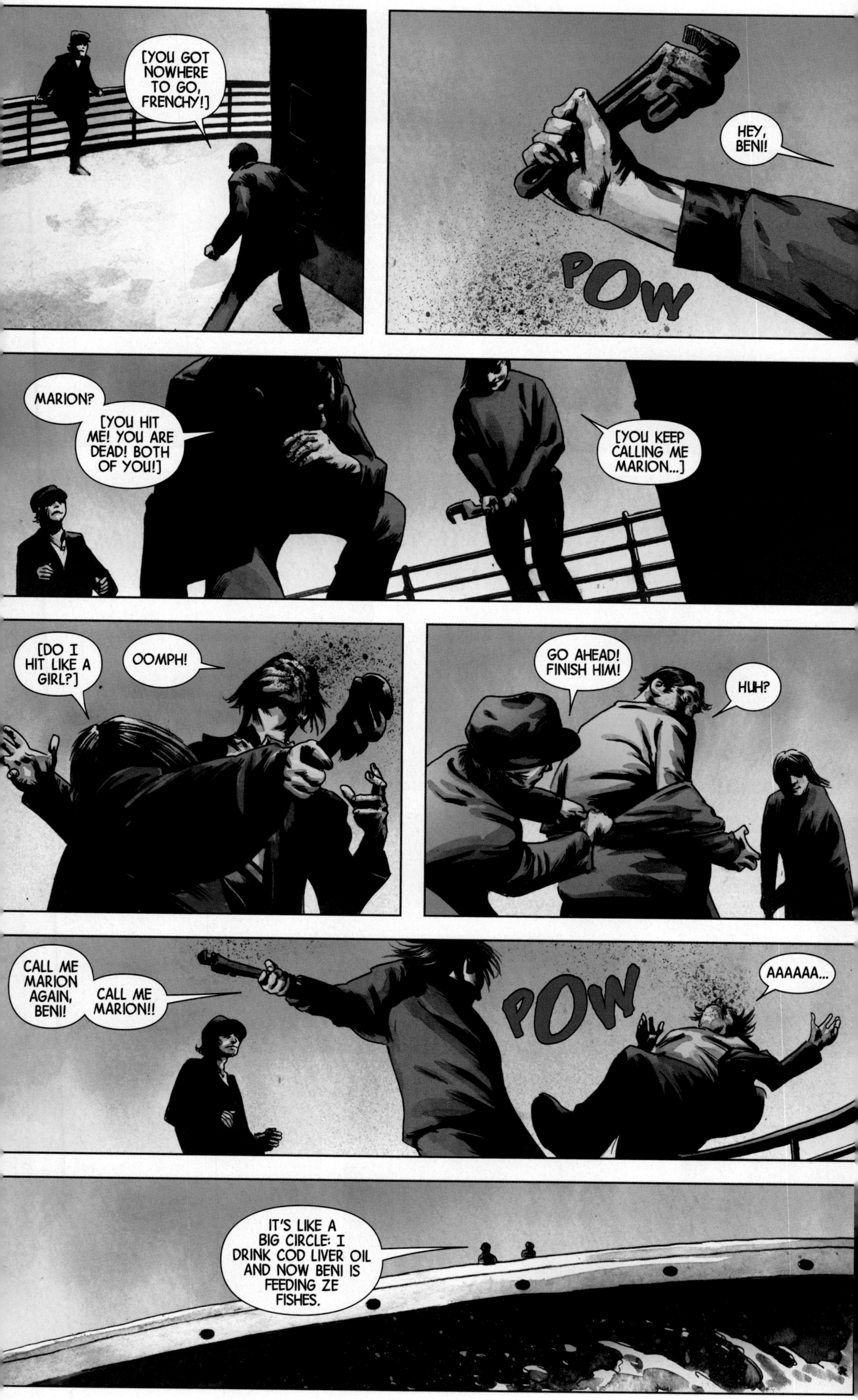

[YOU GOT NOWHERE TO GO, FRENCHY!]
HEY, BENI!
POW
MARION?
[YOU HIT ME! YOU ARE DEAD! BOTH OF YOU!]
[YOU KEEP CALLING ME MARION...]
[DO I HIT LIKE A GIRL?]
OOMPH!
GO AHEAD! FINISH HIM!
HUH?
CALL ME MARION AGAIN, BENI!
CALL ME MARION!!
POW
AAAAAA...
IT'S LIKE A BIG CIRCLE: I DRINK COD LIVER OIL AND NOW BENI IS FEEDING ZE FISHES.

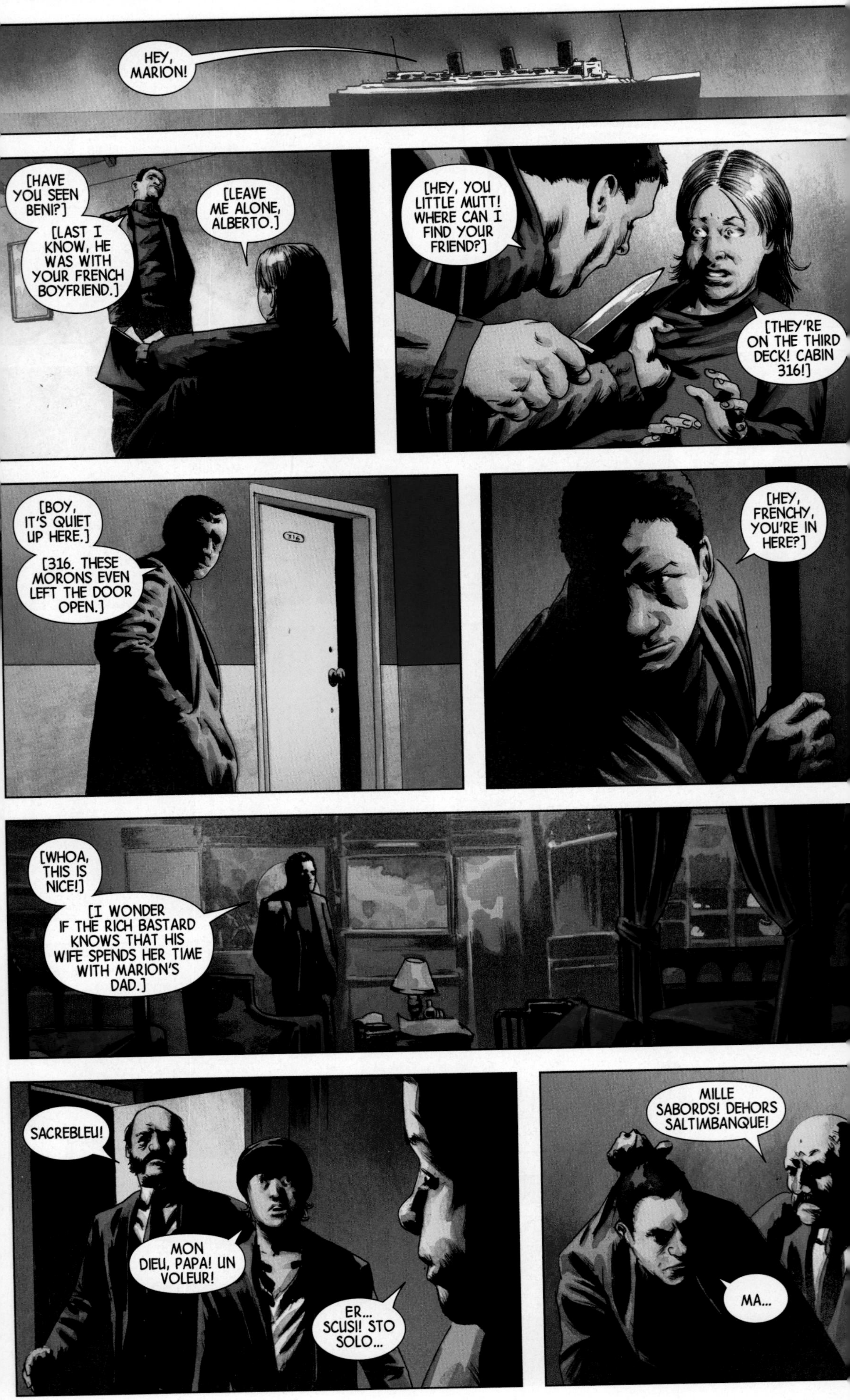

HEY, MARION!
[HAVE YOU SEEN BENI?]
[LAST I KNOW, HE WAS WITH YOUR FRENCH BOYFRIEND.]
[LEAVE ME ALONE, ALBERTO.]
[HEY, YOU LITTLE MUTT! WHERE CAN I FIND YOUR FRIEND?]
[THEY'RE ON THE THIRD DECK! CABIN 316!]
[BOY, IT'S QUIET UP HERE.]
[316. THESE MORONS EVEN LEFT THE DOOR OPEN.]
316
[HEY, FRENCHY, YOU'RE IN HERE?]
[WHOA, THIS IS NICE!]
[I WONDER IF THE RICH BASTARD KNOWS THAT HIS WIFE SPENDS HER TIME WITH MARION'S DAD.]
SACREBLEU!
MON DIEU, PAPA! UN VOLEUR!
ER... SCUSI! STO SOLO...
MILLE SABORDS! DEHORS SALTIMBANQUE!
MA...

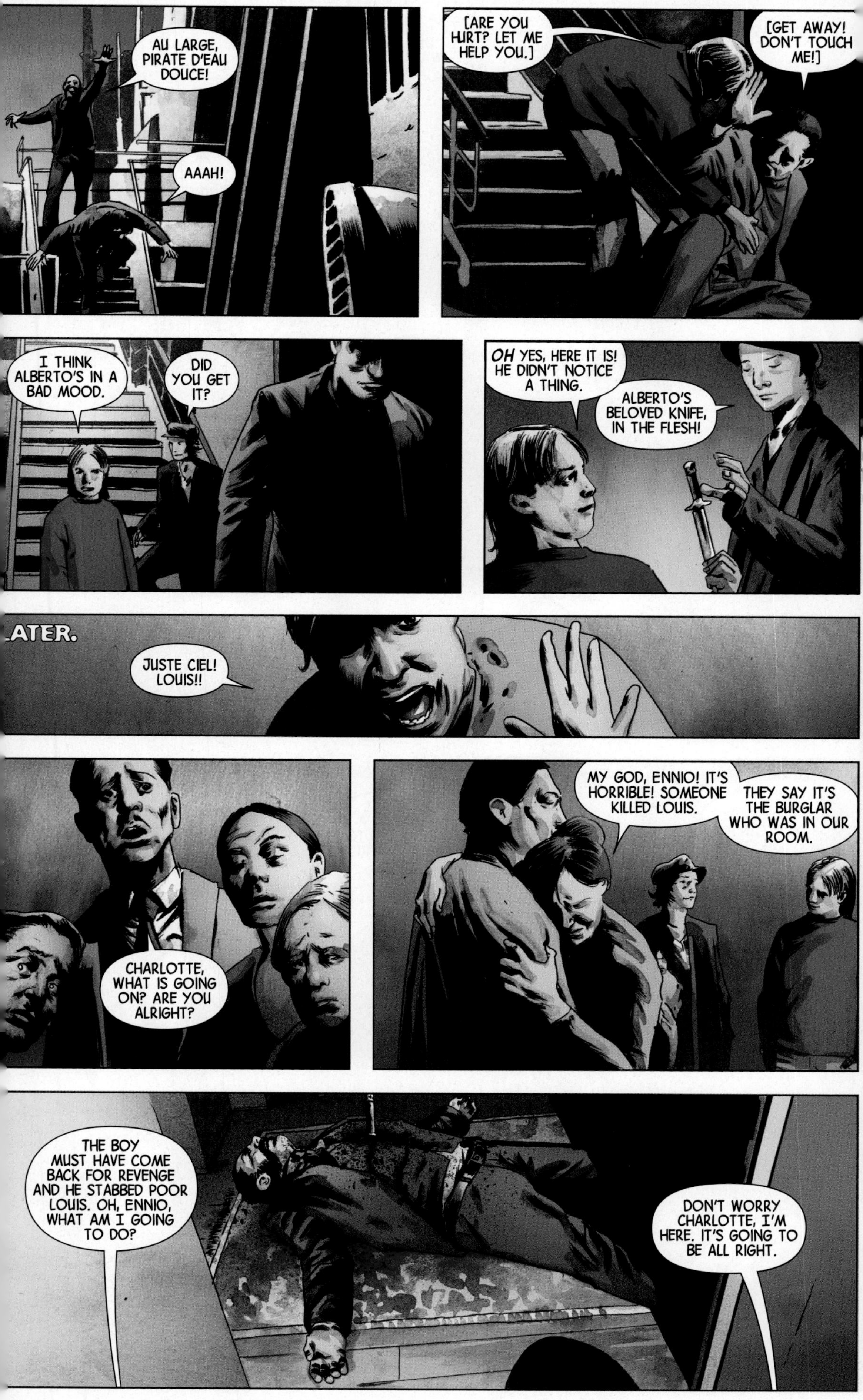
AU LARGE, PIRATE D'EAU DOUCE!
AAAH!
[ARE YOU HURT? LET ME HELP YOU.]
[GET AWAY! DON'T TOUCH ME!]
I THINK ALBERTO'S IN A BAD MOOD.
DID YOU GET IT?
OH YES, HERE IT IS! HE DIDN'T NOTICE A THING.
ALBERTO'S BELOVED KNIFE, IN THE FLESH!
LATER.
JUSTE CIEL! LOUIS!!
CHARLOTTE, WHAT IS GOING ON? ARE YOU ALRIGHT?
MY GOD, ENNIO! IT'S HORRIBLE! SOMEONE KILLED LOUIS.
THEY SAY IT'S THE BURGLAR WHO WAS IN OUR ROOM.
THE BOY MUST HAVE COME BACK FOR REVENGE AND HE STABBED POOR LOUIS. OH, ENNIO, WHAT AM I GOING TO DO?
DON'T WORRY CHARLOTTE, I'M HERE. IT'S GOING TO BE ALL RIGHT.

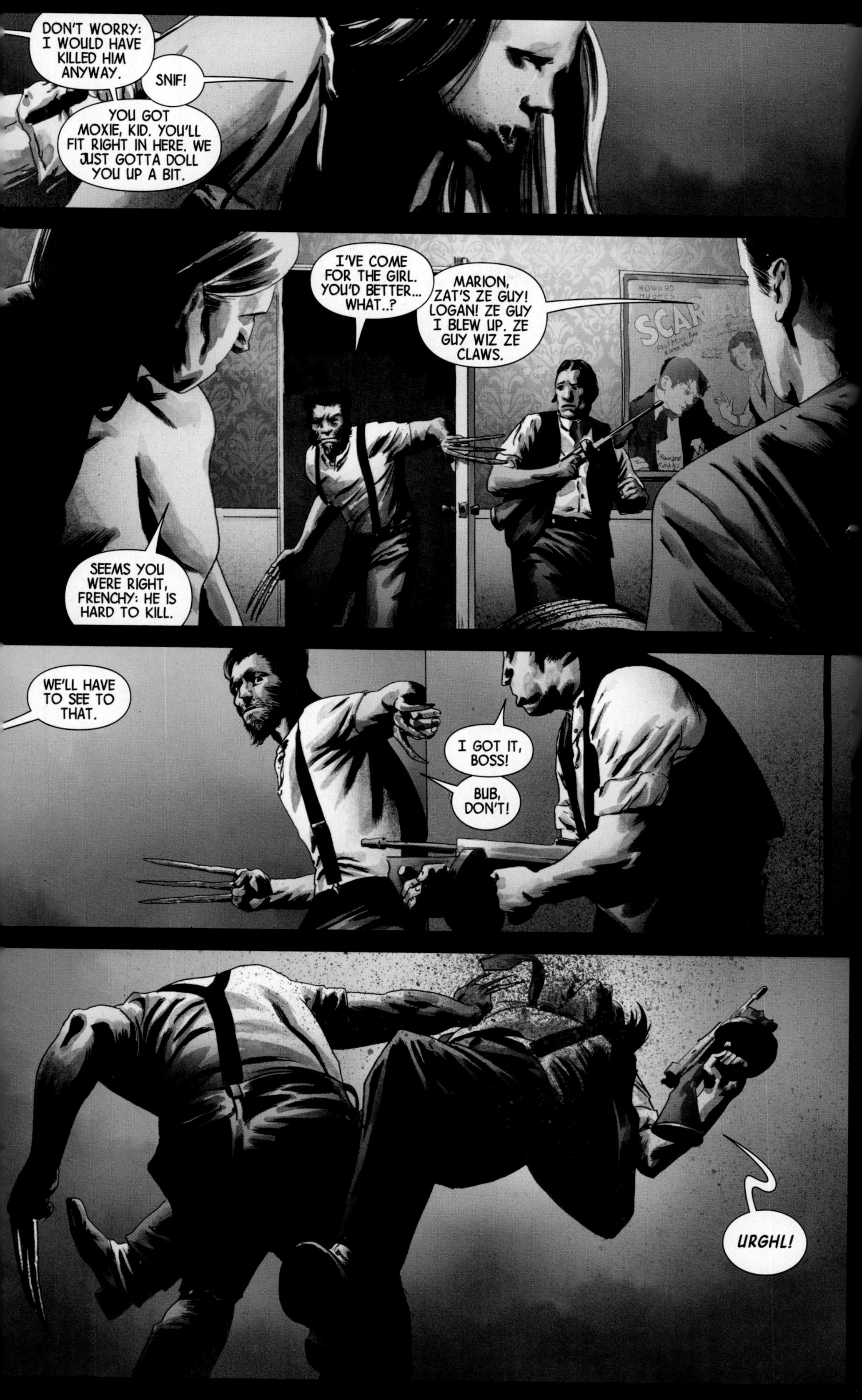
DON'T WORRY: I WOULD HAVE KILLED HIM ANYWAY.
SNIF!
YOU GOT MOXIE, KID. YOU'LL FIT RIGHT IN HERE. WE JUST GOTTA DOLL YOU UP A BIT.
I'VE COME FOR THE GIRL. YOU'D BETTER... WHAT..?
MARION, ZAT'S ZE GUY! LOGAN! ZE GUY I BLEW UP. ZE GUY WIZ ZE CLAWS.
HOWARD HUGHES
SCAR
SEEMS YOU WERE RIGHT, FRENCHY: HE IS HARD TO KILL.
WE'LL HAVE TO SEE TO THAT.
I GOT IT, BOSS!
BUB, DON'T!
URGHL!

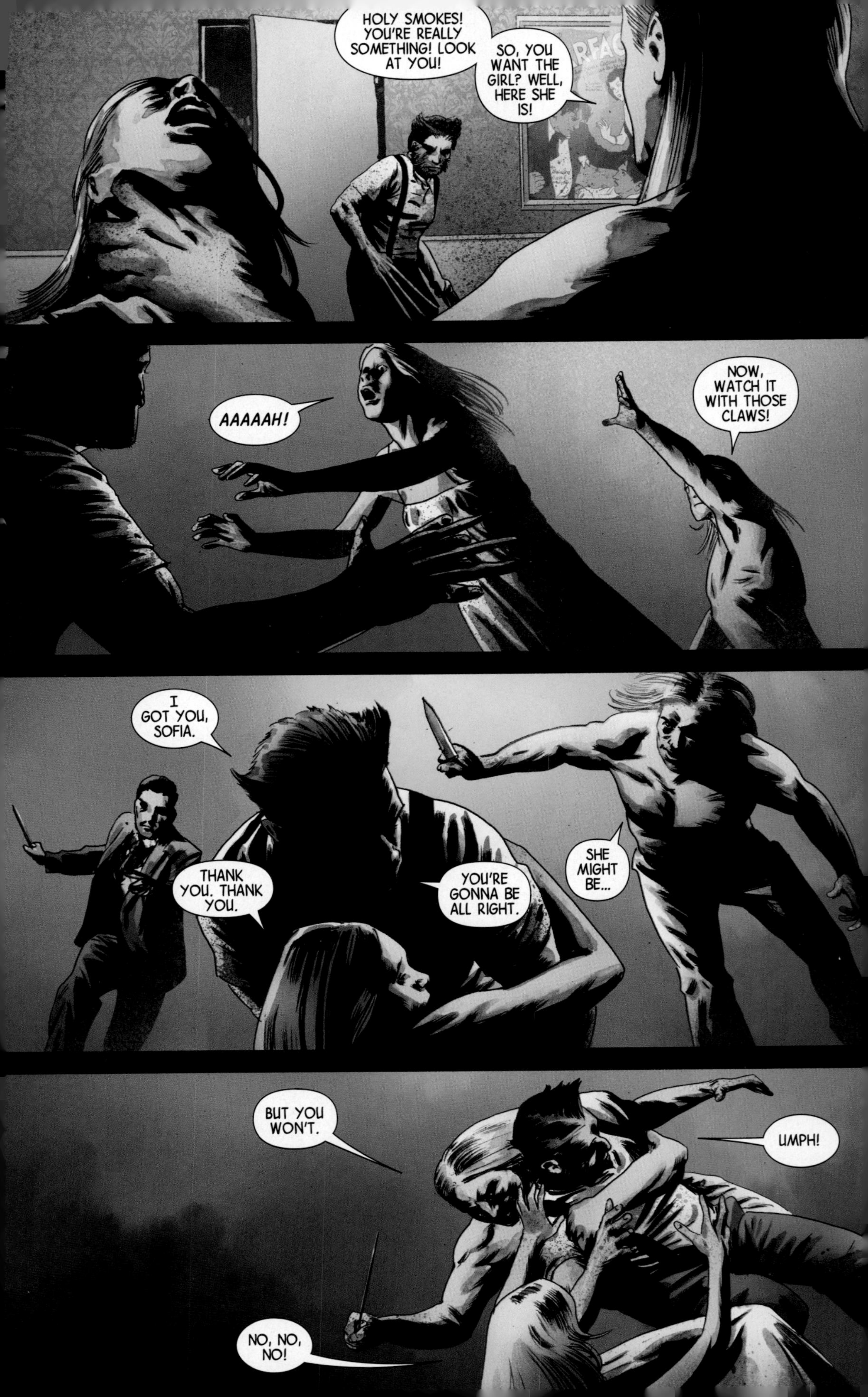
HOLY SMOKES! YOU'RE REALLY SOMETHING! LOOK AT YOU!
SO, YOU WANT THE GIRL? WELL, HERE SHE IS!
AAAAAH!
NOW, WATCH IT WITH THOSE CLAWS!
I GOT YOU, SOFIA.
THANK YOU. THANK YOU.
YOU'RE GONNA BE ALL RIGHT.
SHE MIGHT BE...
BUT YOU WON'T.
UMPH!
NO, NO, NO!

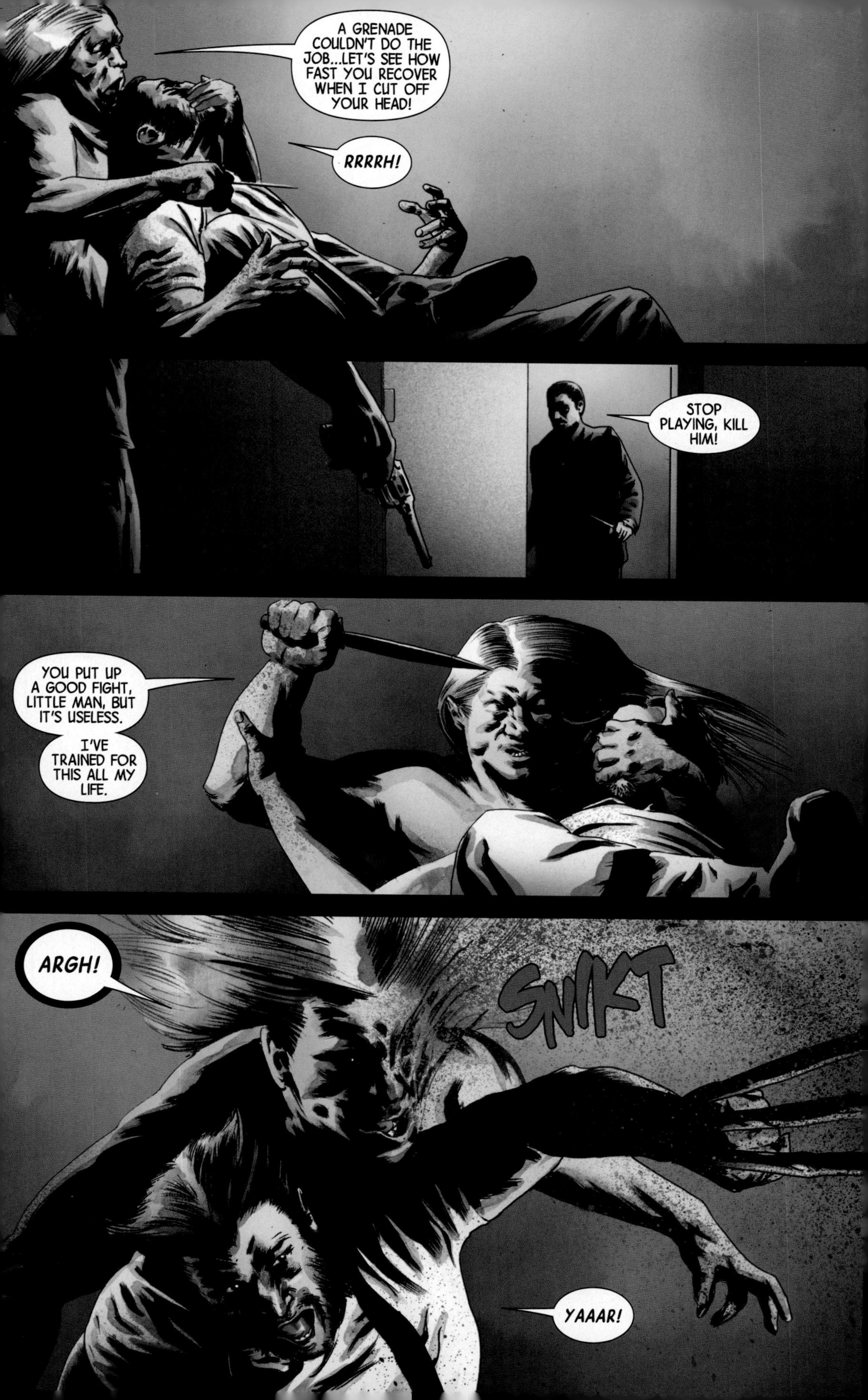
A GRENADE COULDN'T DO THE JOB...LET'S SEE HOW FAST YOU RECOVER WHEN I CUT OFF YOUR HEAD!
RRRRH!
STOP PLAYING, KILL HIM!
YOU PUT UP A GOOD FIGHT, LITTLE MAN, BUT IT'S USELESS.
I'VE TRAINED FOR THIS ALL MY LIFE.
ARGH!
SNIKT
YAAAR!

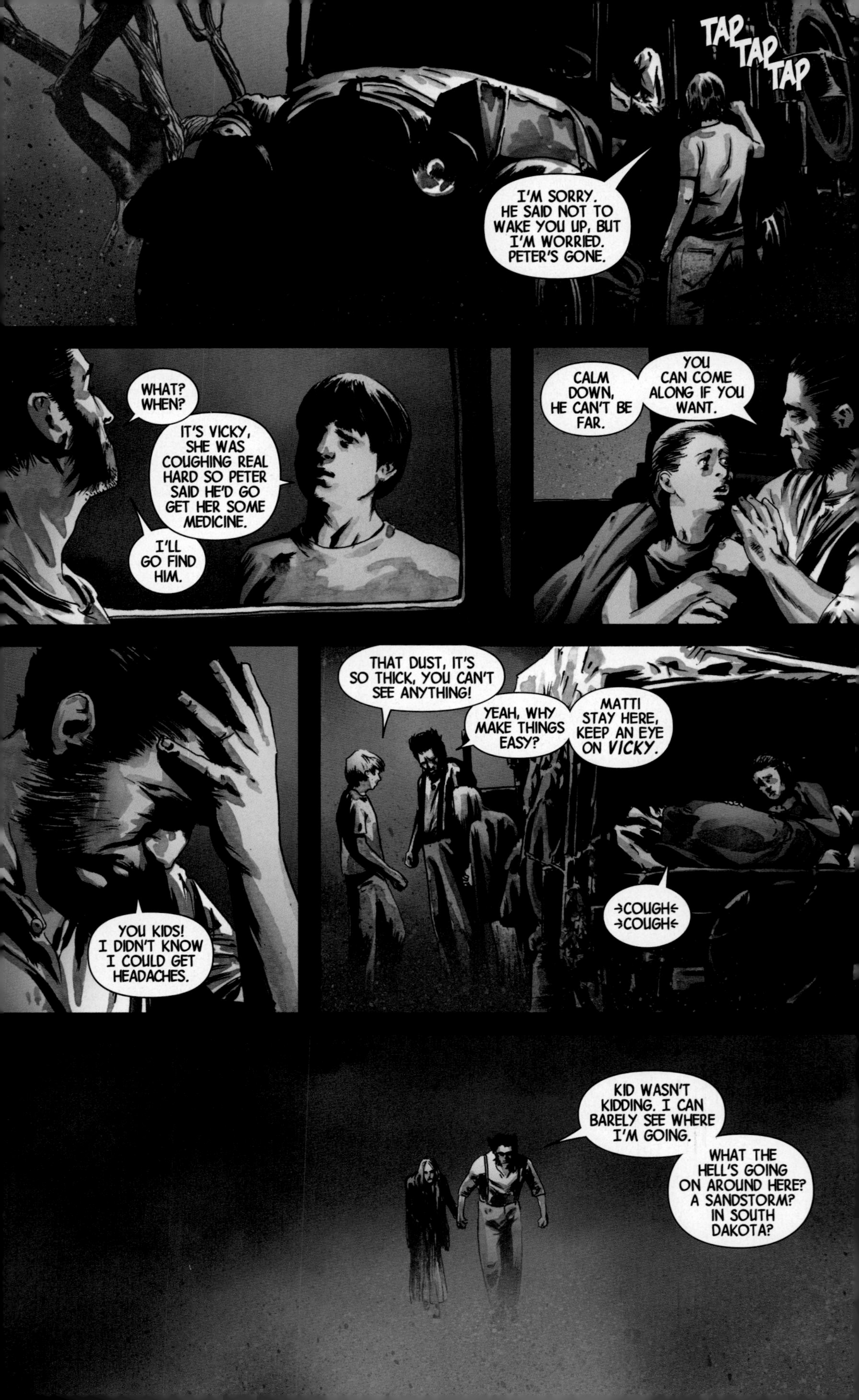
TAP TAP TAP
I'M SORRY. HE SAID NOT TO WAKE YOU UP, BUT I'M WORRIED. PETER'S GONE.
WHAT? WHEN?
IT'S VICKY, SHE WAS COUGHING REAL HARD SO PETER SAID HE'D GO GET HER SOME MEDICINE.
I'LL GO FIND HIM.
CALM DOWN, HE CAN'T BE FAR.
YOU CAN COME ALONG IF YOU WANT.
YOU KIDS! I DIDN'T KNOW I COULD GET HEADACHES.
THAT DUST, IT'S SO THICK, YOU CAN'T SEE ANYTHING!
YEAH, WHY MAKE THINGS EASY?
MATTI STAY HERE, KEEP AN EYE ON VICKY.
COUGH COUGH
KID WASN'T KIDDING. I CAN BARELY SEE WHERE I'M GOING.
WHAT THE HELL'S GOING ON AROUND HERE? A SANDSTORM? IN SOUTH DAKOTA?

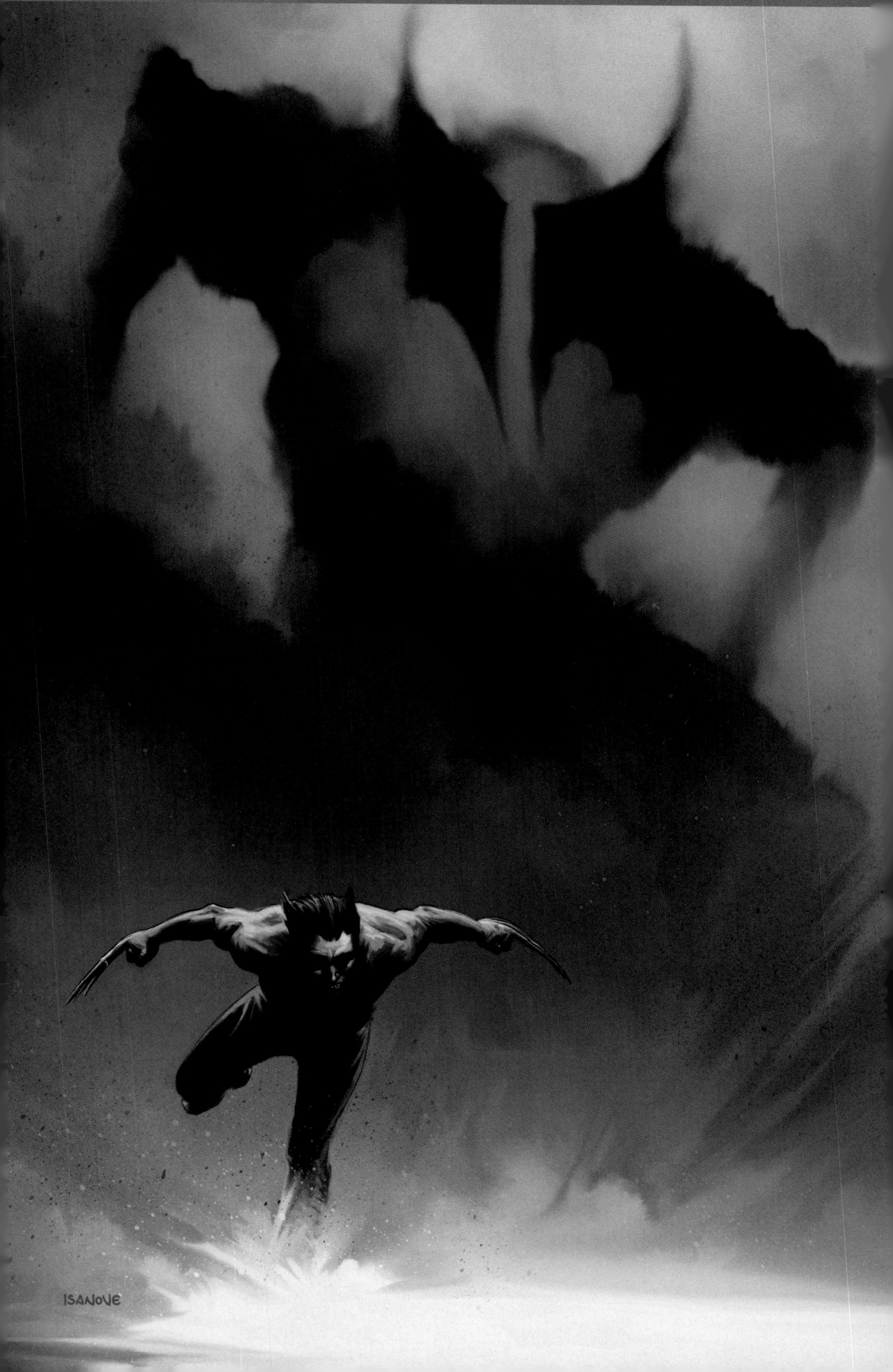
ISANOVE

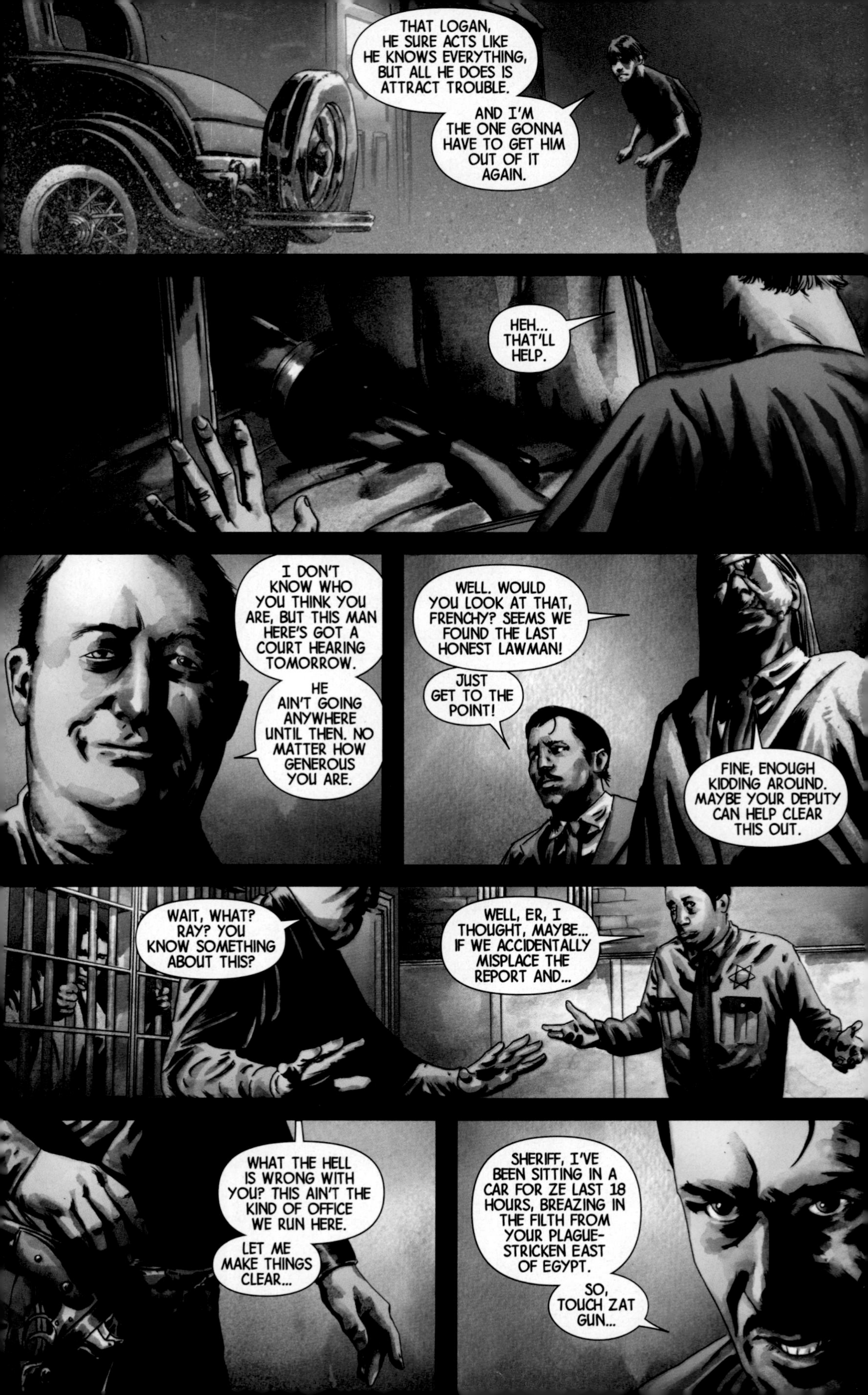
THAT LOGAN, HE SURE ACTS LIKE HE KNOWS EVERYTHING, BUT ALL HE DOES IS ATTRACT TROUBLE.
AND I'M THE ONE GONNA HAVE TO GET HIM OUT OF IT AGAIN.
HEH... THAT'LL HELP.
I DON'T KNOW WHO YOU THINK YOU ARE, BUT THIS MAN HERE'S GOT A COURT HEARING TOMORROW.
HE AIN'T GOING ANYWHERE UNTIL THEN. NO MATTER HOW GENEROUS YOU ARE.
WELL. WOULD YOU LOOK AT THAT, FRENCHY? SEEMS WE FOUND THE LAST HONEST LAWMAN!
JUST GET TO THE POINT!
FINE, ENOUGH KIDDING AROUND. MAYBE YOUR DEPUTY CAN HELP CLEAR THIS OUT.
WAIT, WHAT? RAY? YOU KNOW SOMETHING ABOUT THIS?
WELL, ER, I THOUGHT, MAYBE... IF WE ACCIDENTALLY MISPLACE THE REPORT AND...
WHAT THE HELL IS WRONG WITH YOU? THIS AIN'T THE KIND OF OFFICE WE RUN HERE.
LET ME MAKE THINGS CLEAR...
SHERIFF, I'VE BEEN SITTING IN A CAR FOR ZE LAST 18 HOURS, BREAZING IN THE FILTH FROM YOUR PLAGUE-STRICKEN EAST OF EGYPT.
SO, TOUCH ZAT GUN...

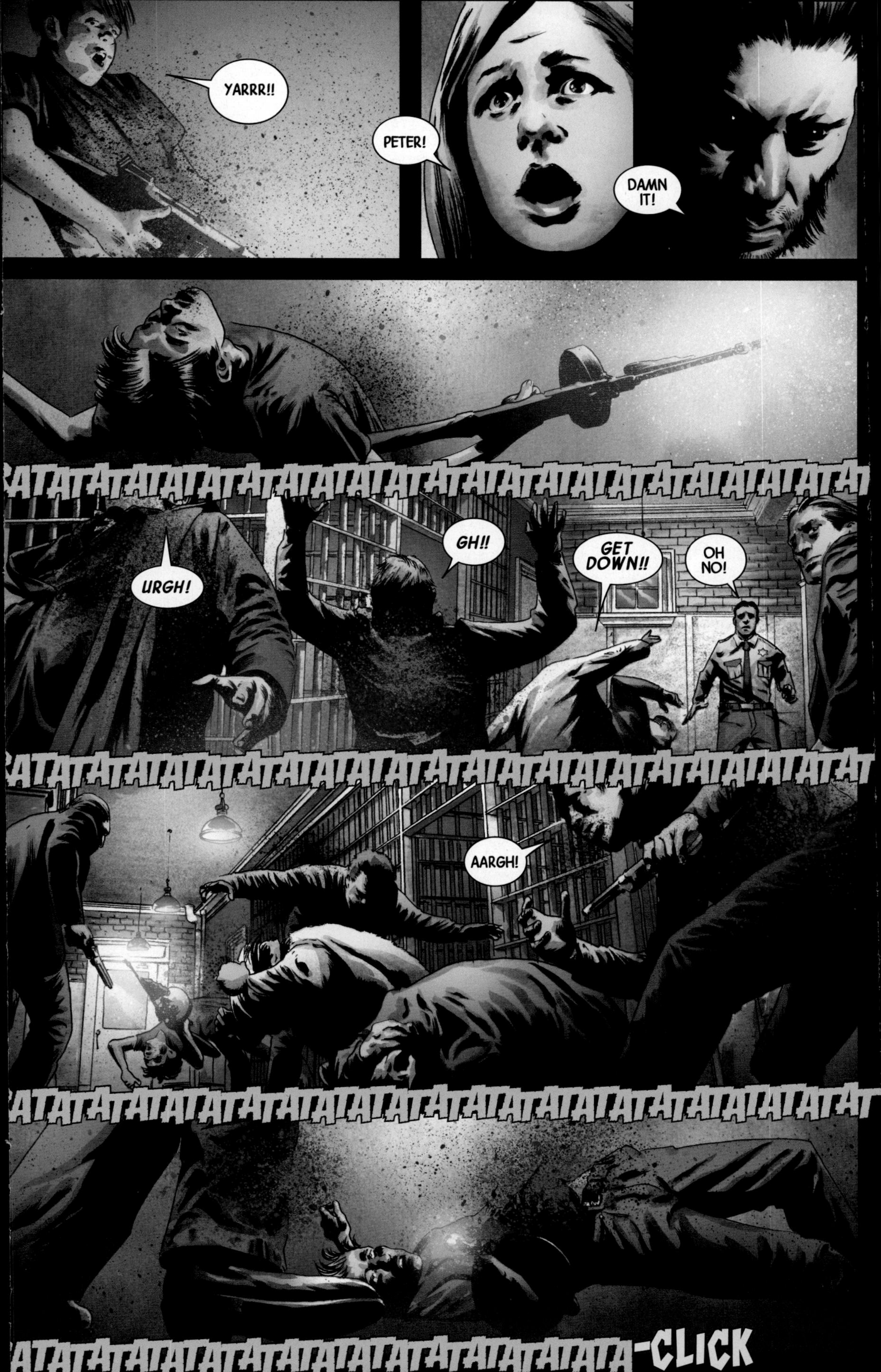
YARRR!!
PETER!
DAMN IT!
TATATATATATATATATATATATATATATATATATATATATAT
URGH!
GH!!
GET DOWN!!
OH NO!
TATATATATATATATATATATATATATATATATATATATATAT
AARGH!
TATATATATATATATATATATATATATATATATATATATATAT
TATATATATATATATATATATATATATATATATATATA-CLICK

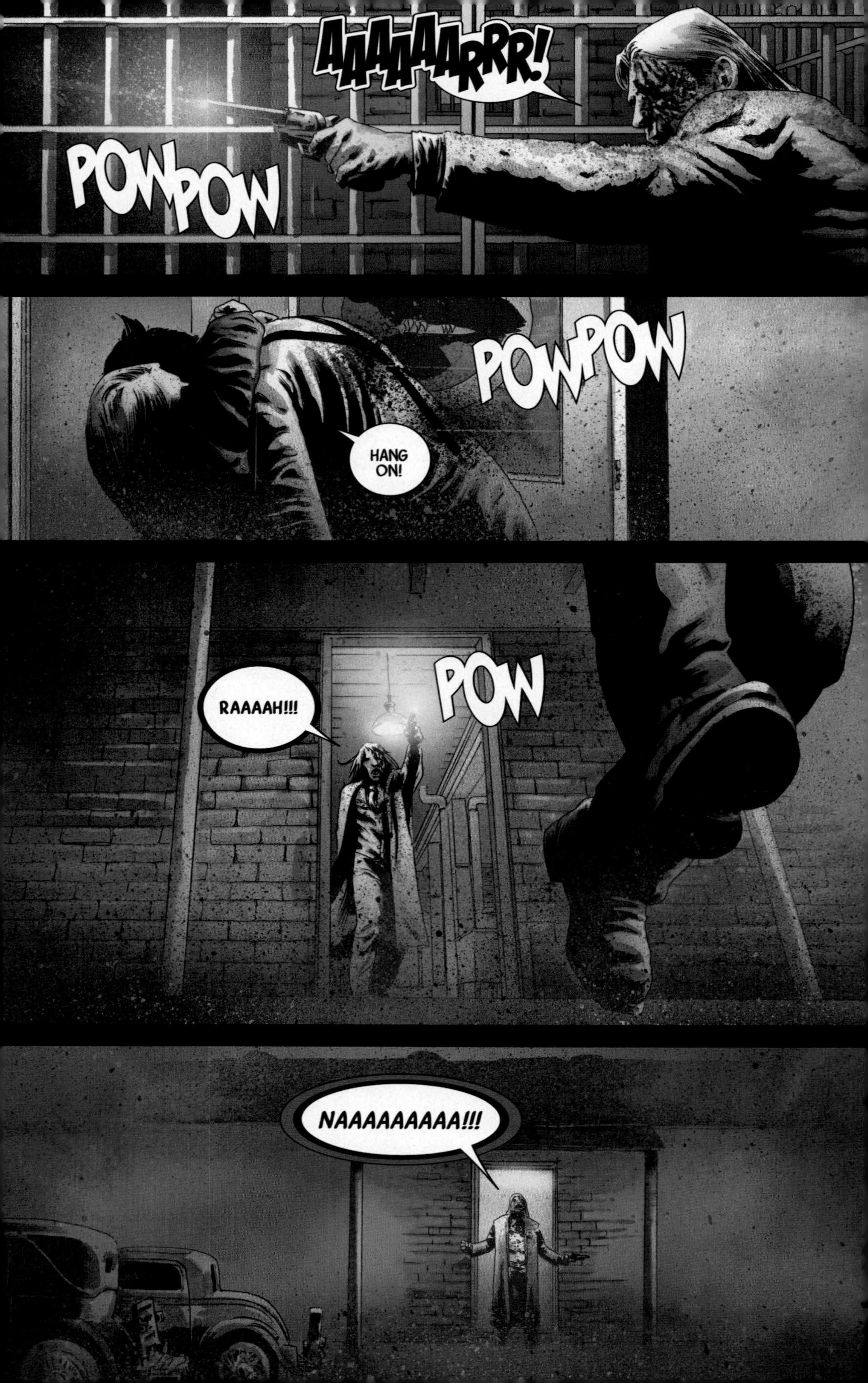
AAAAAARRR!
POWPOW
POWPOW
HANG ON!
RAAAAH!!!
POW
NAAAAAAAAA!!!

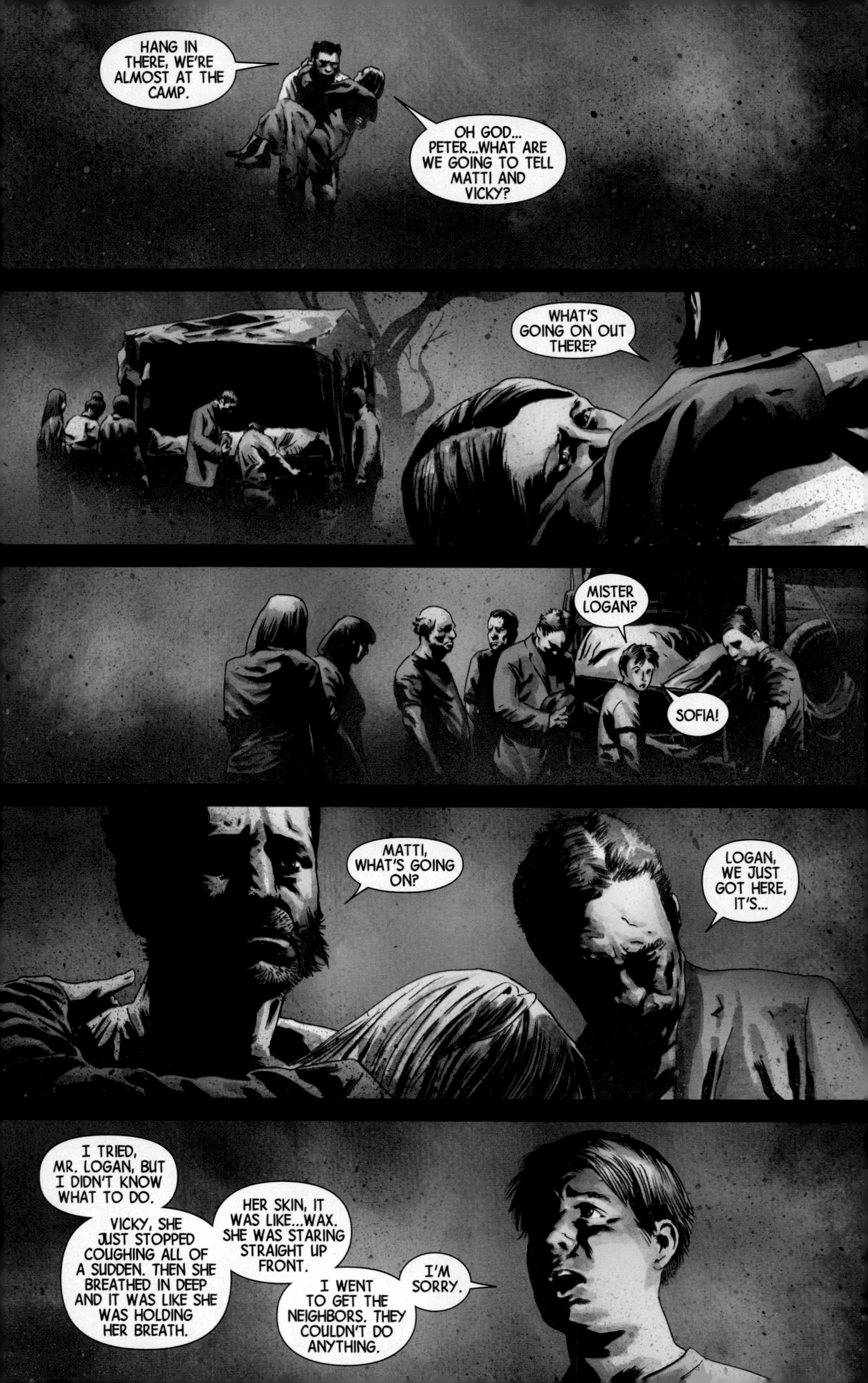
HANG IN THERE, WE'RE ALMOST AT THE CAMP.
OH GOD... PETER...WHAT ARE WE GOING TO TELL MATTI AND VICKY?
WHAT'S GOING ON OUT THERE?
MISTER LOGAN?
SOFIA!
MATTI, WHAT'S GOING ON?
LOGAN, WE JUST GOT HERE, IT'S...
I TRIED, MR. LOGAN, BUT I DIDN'T KNOW WHAT TO DO.
VICKY, SHE JUST STOPPED COUGHING ALL OF A SUDDEN. THEN SHE BREATHED IN DEEP AND IT WAS LIKE SHE WAS HOLDING HER BREATH.
HER SKIN, IT WAS LIKE...WAX. SHE WAS STARING STRAIGHT UP FRONT.
I WENT TO GET THE NEIGHBORS. THEY COULDN'T DO ANYTHING.
I'M SORRY.

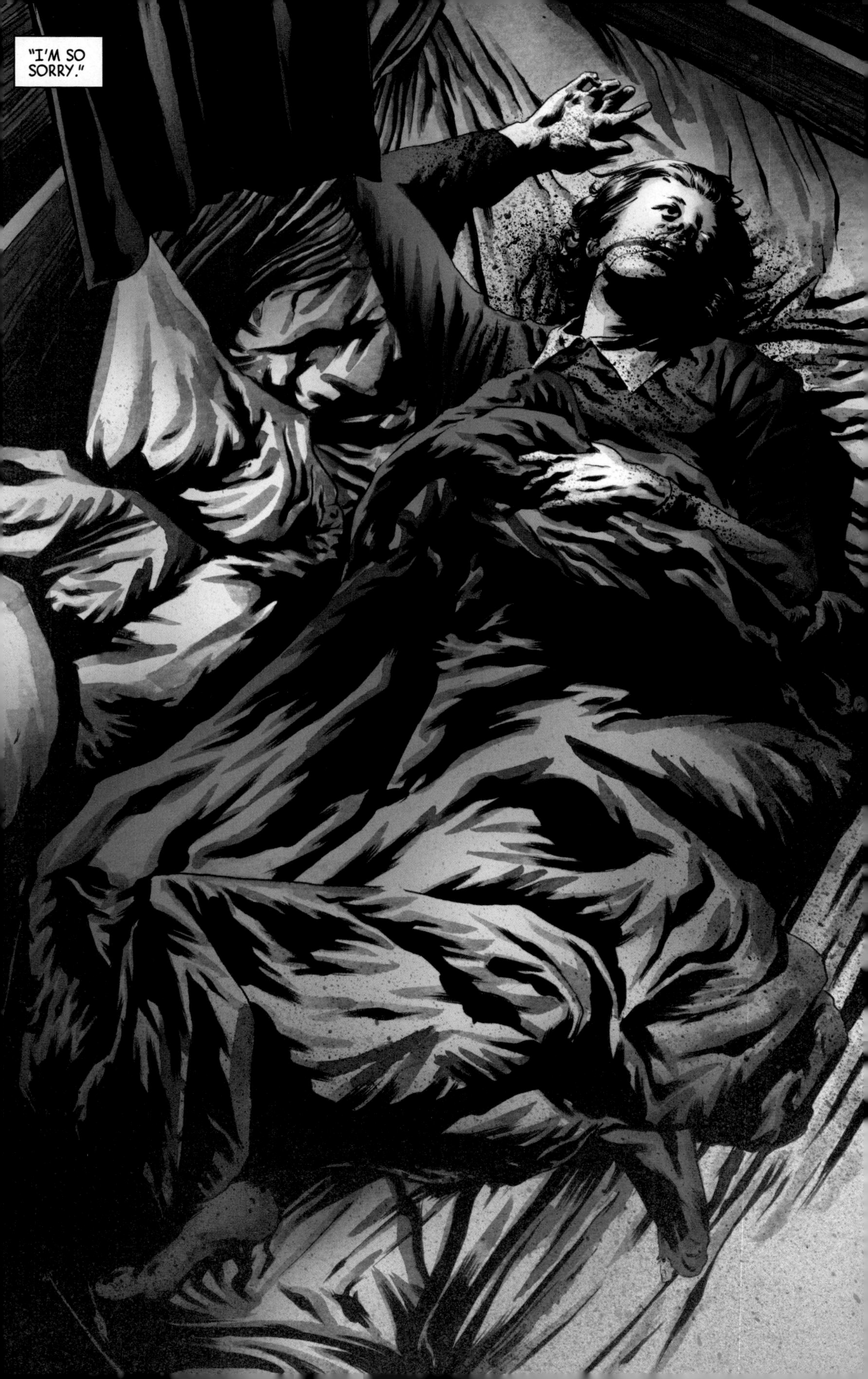
"I'M SO SORRY."

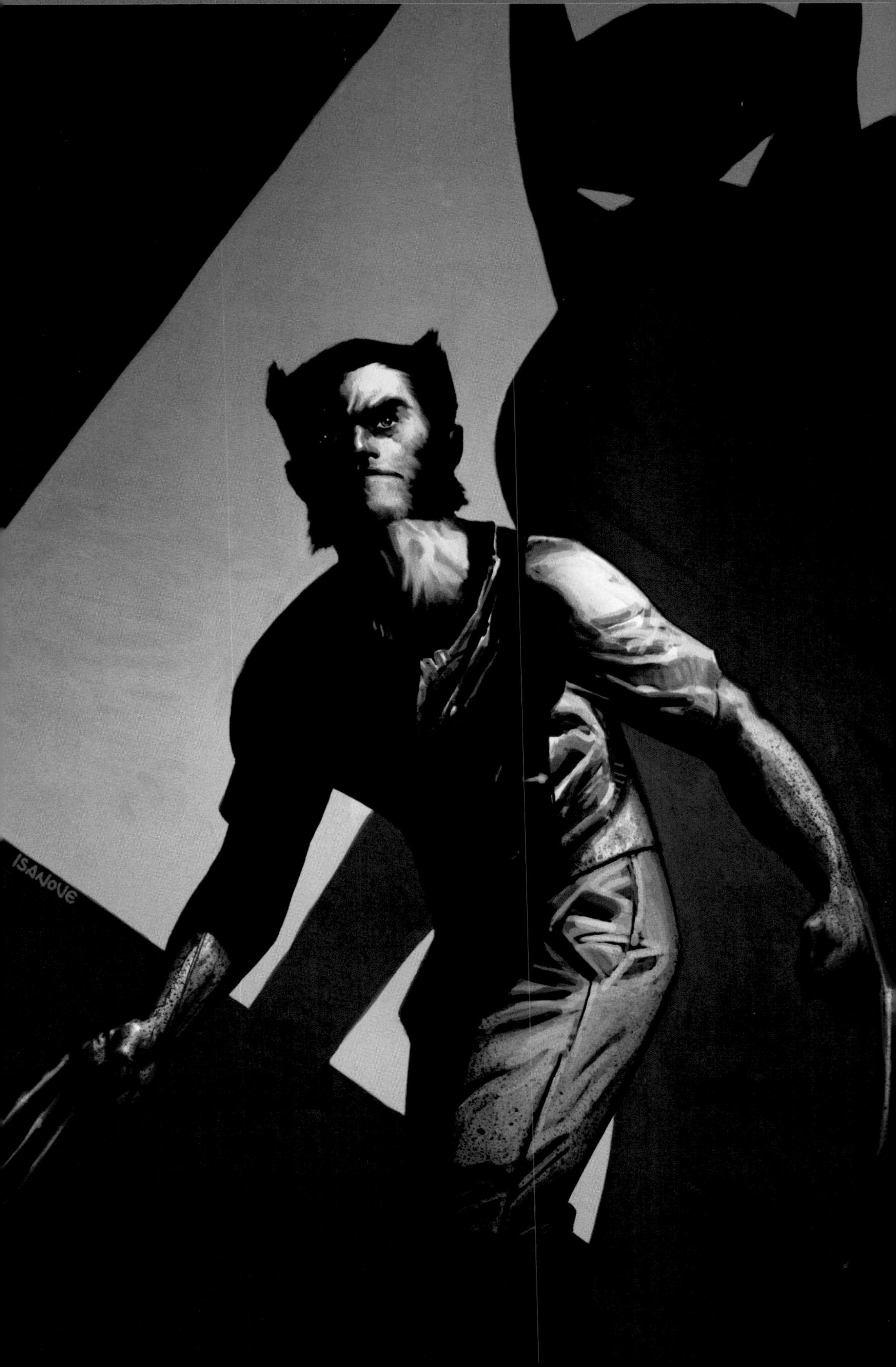
ISANOVE

NOVEMBER 13, 1933.
RAPID CREEK MOTEL,
SOUTH DAKOTA.

MOTEL

MORNING. I GOT US SOME SINKERS FOR BREAKFAST.

GOT A NEWSPAPER, TOO.

THANKS TO THE SANDSTORM, THE FIASCO AT THE POLICE STATION DIDN'T MAKE IT ABOVE THE FOLD.

WHAT'S THAT SMELL?

IT'S ZE KID'S GUT WOUND. STINKS TO HIGH HEAVEN.

DON'T SHUT ZE DOOR ALL THE WAY, LET SOME AIR IN.

DID YOU CALL CHICAGO?

YEAH...WE MAY NOT BE BIG NEWS HERE, BUT STILL THEY AIN'T HAPPY ABOUT THIS MESS.

OUR MARCHING ORDERS ARE TO GET BACK THERE PRONTO.

NO.

WE'RE NOT GOING ANYWHERE...

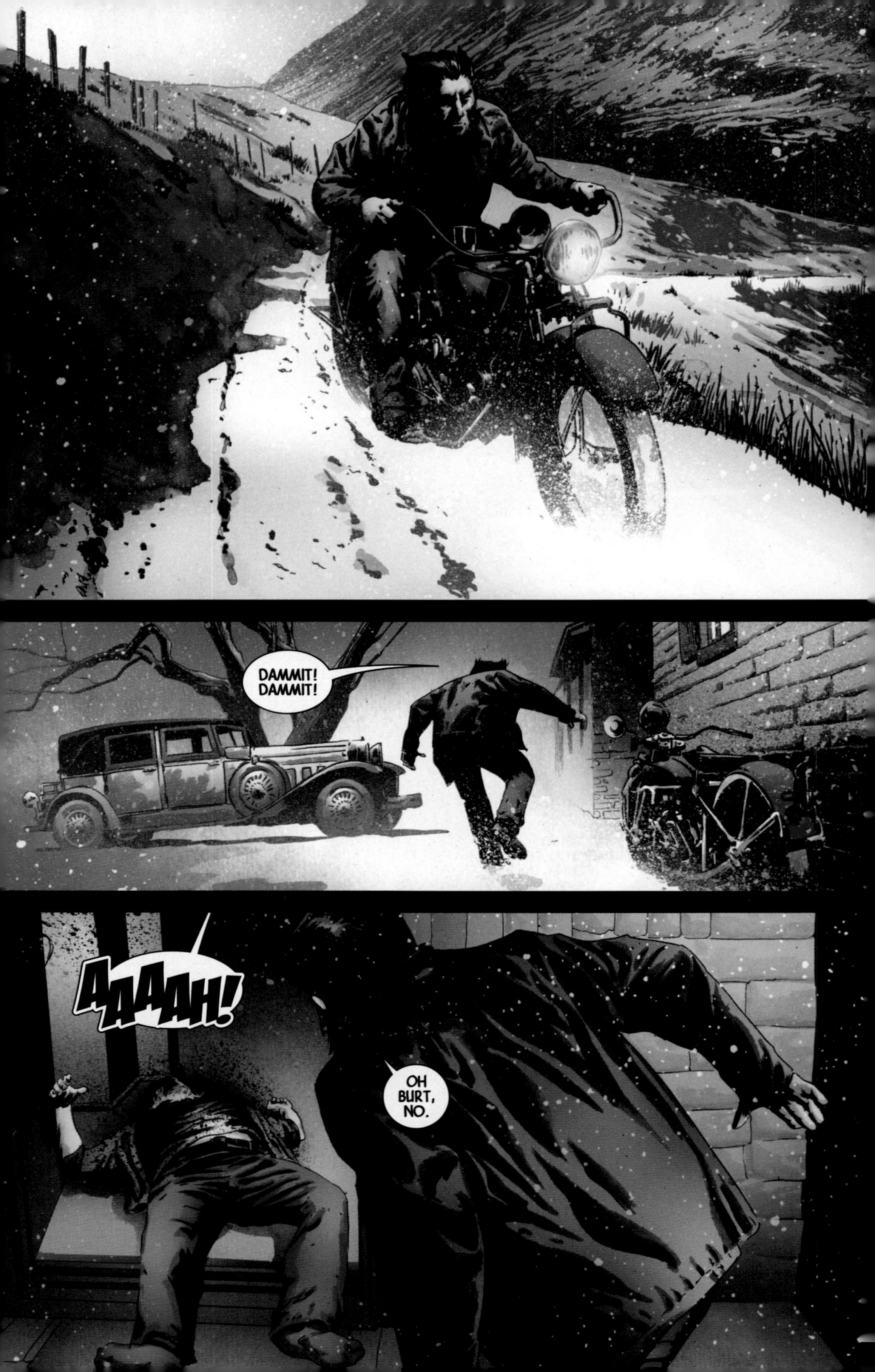
DAMMIT! DAMMIT!
AAAAH!
OH BURT, NO.

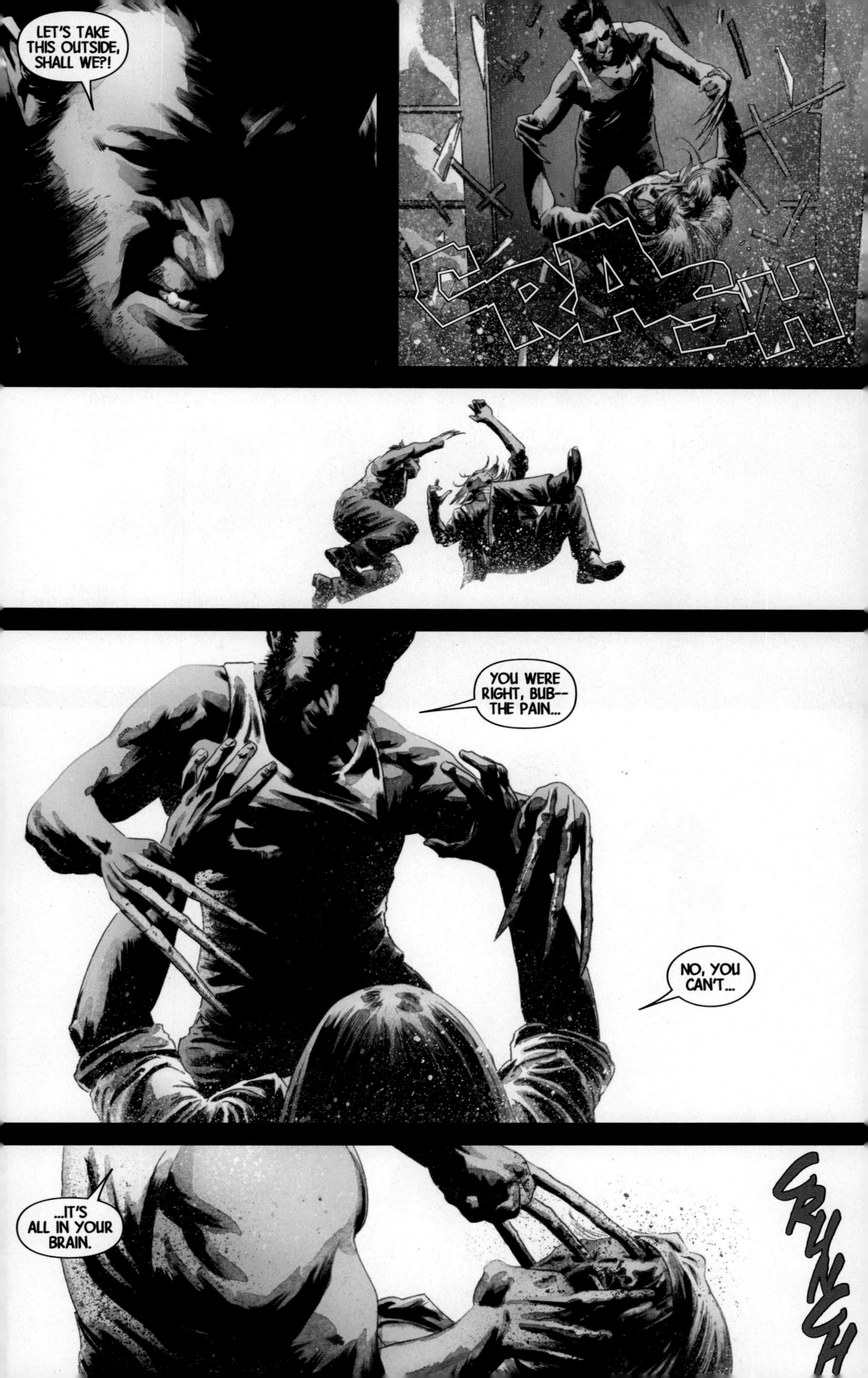
LET'S TAKE THIS OUTSIDE, SHALL WE?!
CRASH
YOU WERE RIGHT, BUB-- THE PAIN...
NO, YOU CAN'T...
...IT'S ALL IN YOUR BRAIN.
CRUNCH

END.

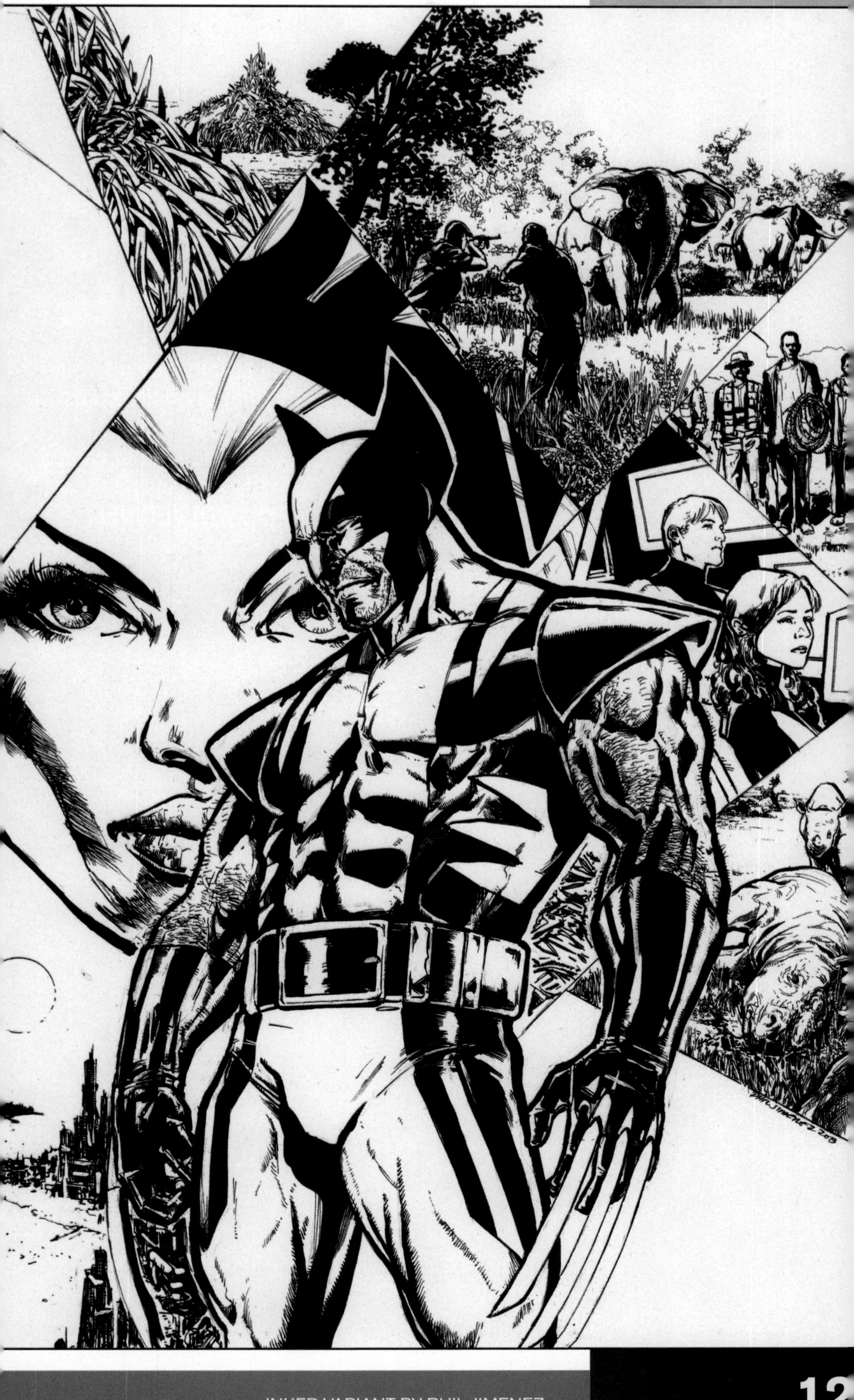

INKED VARIANT BY PHIL JIMENEZ

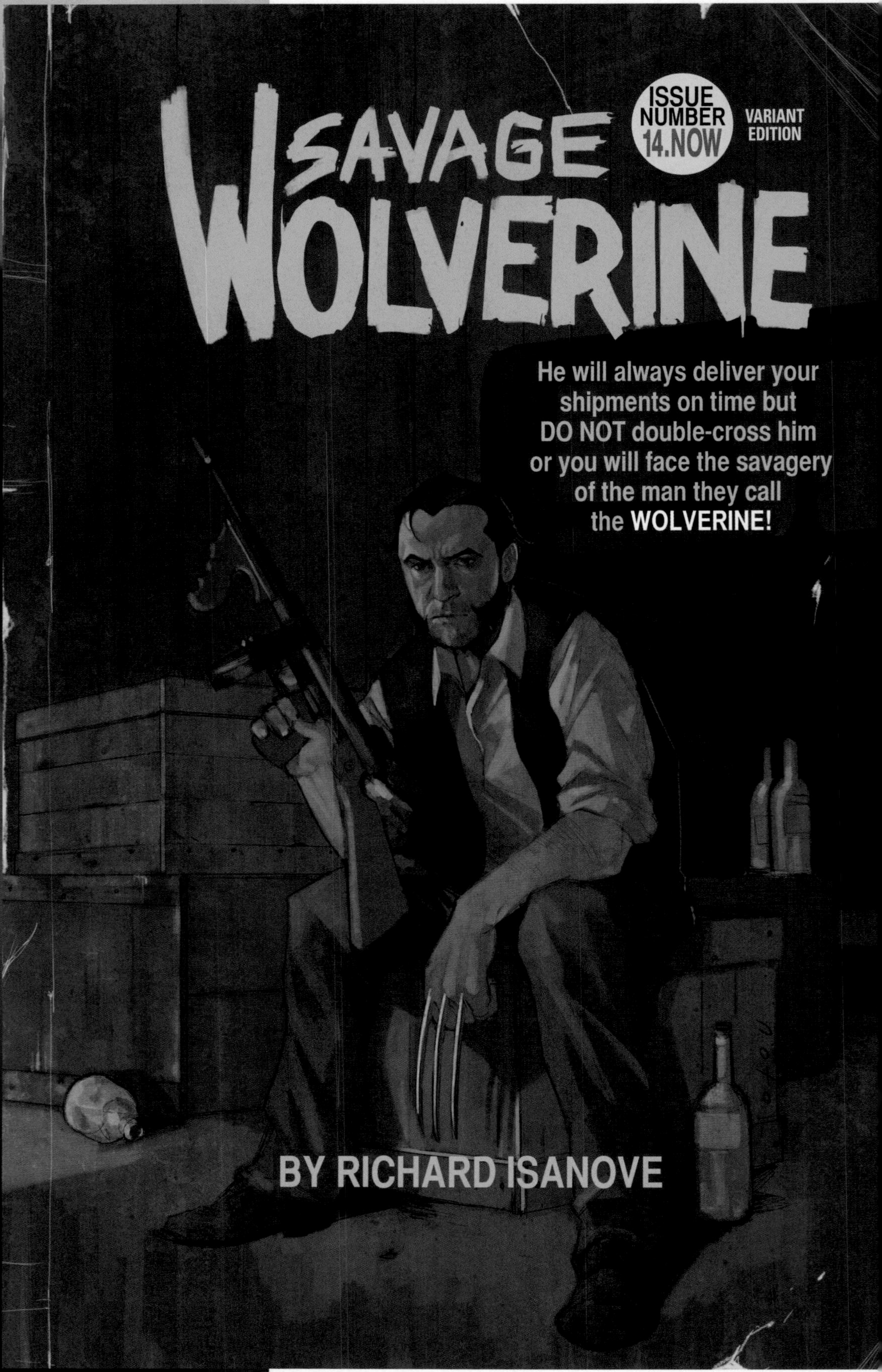
SAVAGE WOLVERINE
ISSUE NUMBER 14.NOW
VARIANT EDITION
He will always deliver your shipments on time but DO NOT double-cross him or you will face the savagery of the man they call the WOLVERINE!
BY RICHARD ISANOVE

VARIANT BY PHIL NOTO

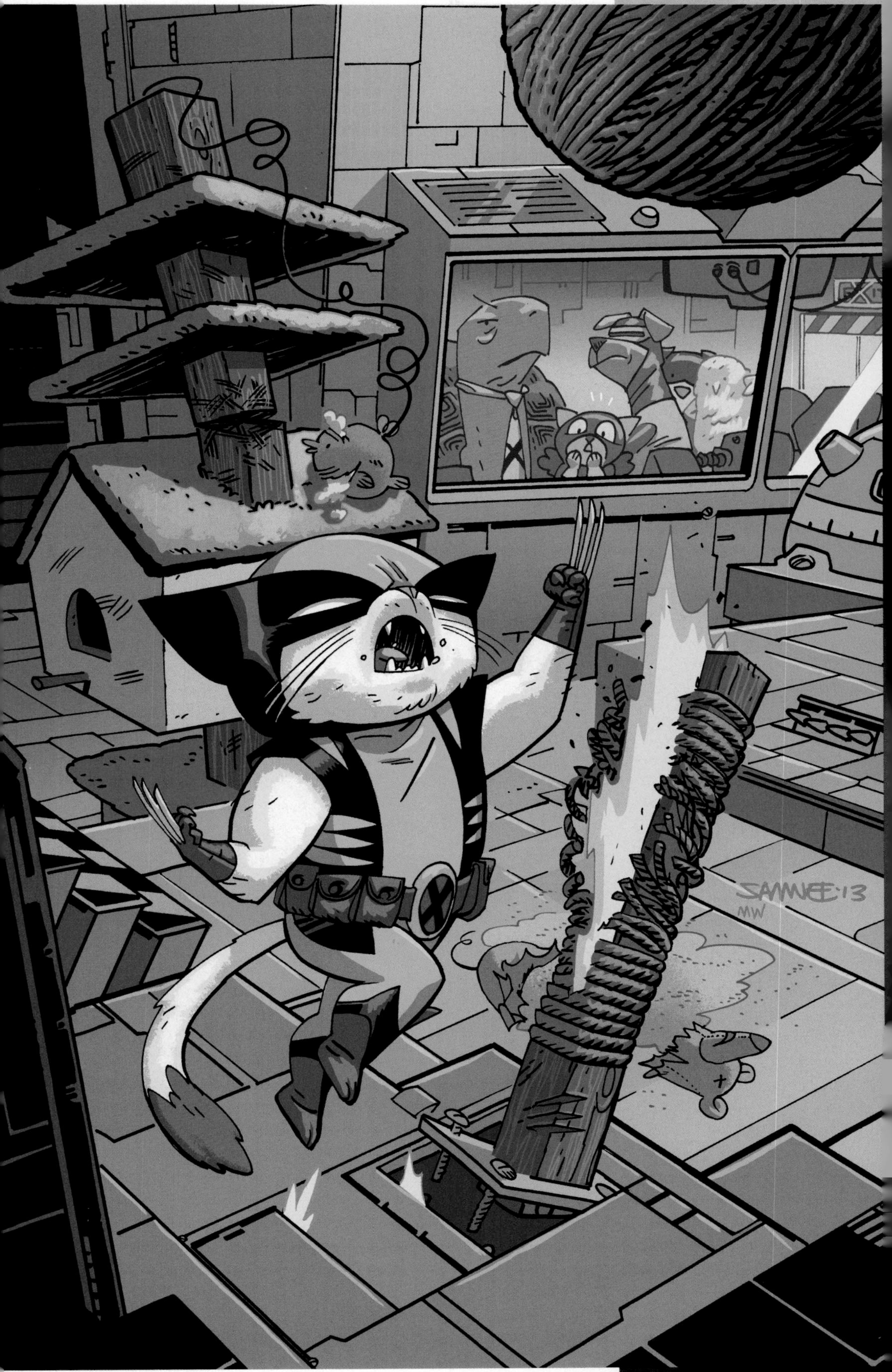
SAMNEE '13
MW

ANIMAL VARIANT BY CHRIS SAMNEE & MATTHEW WILSON

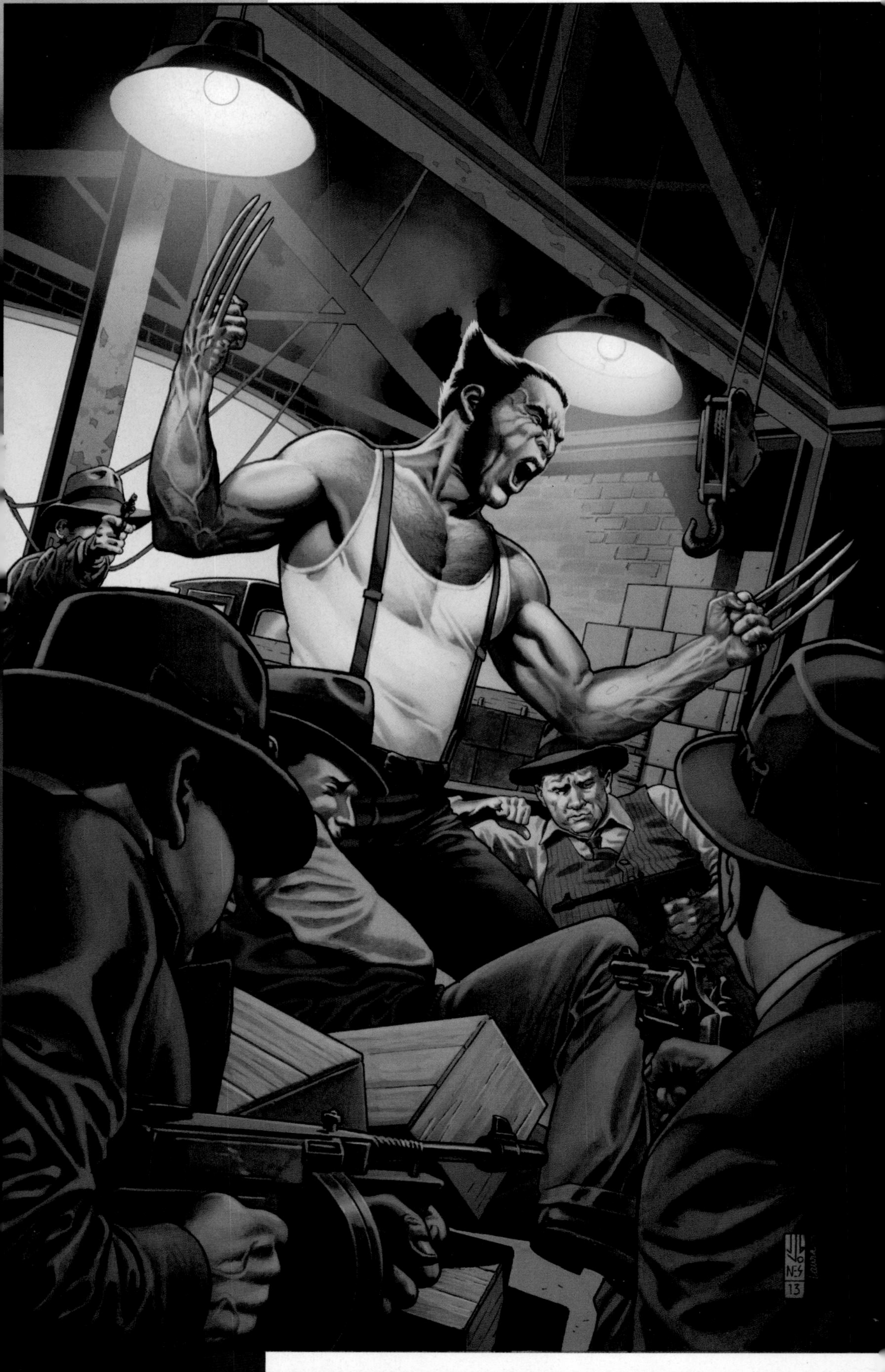
JG JONES 13

VARIANT BY J.G. JONES

"...UNIQUELY WRITTEN...NEARLY PERFECT" – *SuperHeroHype.com*

"A GORGEOUS BOOK." – *WeeklyComicBookReview.com*

"A gorgeous book to look at." — WeeklyComicBookReview.com
FRANK CHO
SAVAGE WOLVERINE
SNIKT
KILL ISLAND
AR
MARVEL NOW!

SAVAGE WOLVERINE VOL. 1: KILL ISLAND

978-0-7851-6722-8 • JAN140802

[redacted]

TO REDEEM YOUR CODE FOR A FREE DIGITAL COPY:

1. GO TO MARVEL.COM/REDEEM. OFFER EXPIRES ON 6/16/16.
2. FOLLOW THE ON-SCREEN INSTRUCTIONS TO REDEEM YOUR DIGITAL COPY.
3. LAUNCH THE MARVEL COMICS APP TO READ YOUR COMIC NOW!
4. YOUR DIGITAL COPY WILL BE FOUND UNDER THE *MY COMICS* TAB.
5. READ & ENJOY!

YOUR FREE DIGITAL COPY WILL BE AVAILABL

MARVEL COMICS APP FOR APPLE® iOS DEVICES

MARVEL COMICS AP FOR ANDROID™ DEVI

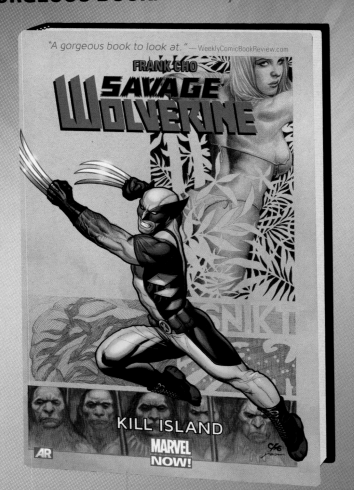